GARDEN LIBRARY
PLANTING FIELDS ARBORETUM

D1489548

A Guide to The Nature Conservancy's Preserves in Wisconsin

Acknowledgments

Many people had a hand in putting this book together. The Nature Conservancy would like to acknowledge them here and thank them for their invaluable assistance. Thanks go to Nancy Braker, Becky Isenring, Ken Lange, and Dr. Stan Temple for sharing their scientific expertise in the proofreading of this book. We are also grateful for the many hours that Nancy Braker, Kathie Brock, Steve Richter and Jim Welsh spent revising preserve maps for use by the artist in creating the maps for this book. Thanks also go to Tom and Kathie Brock for lending their book publishing experience to this project. Finally, The Nature Conservancy would like to thank all the photographers who donated their beautiful images for use in this book.

Some of the material used in this book was taken from an earlier Wisconsin Chapter preserve guide, *The Places We Save* (1988). Thanks go to Mary M. Maher and the staff at Mixed Media, Madison, Wisconsin, who wrote and coordinated the production of that book.

For more information about The Nature Conservancy's work in Wisconsin contact: The Nature Conservancy, Wisconsin Chapter, 633 W. Main St., Madison, WI 53703.

© Wisconsin Chapter of The Nature Conservancy, 1997
Photography © 1997: Jeff Richter, front cover; Scott W. Mulcahy, 4, 27, 45, 85; Harold E. Malde, 6, 43, 51, 62, 72, 82, 86, 92; Stephen J. Lang, 8, 58, 71, 100; The Nature Conservancy, 11, 13, 29, 37, 56, 76, 93, 102, 117; Nancy Braker, 15, 46; Matt Sanford, 16; Lawrence A. Michael, 19,; Gerald H. Emmerich, Jr., 23, 68, 77, 80; Anita Temple, 25; Robert A. Kleppin, 28, 78; Tom Fosdal, 32; Thomas A. Meyer, 41, 57, 90, 105, 110; Rob Baller, 66; Mike Grimm, 88; Michael-John Jaeger, 106; Dave Westover, back cover, 42, 50, 96, 97.

NorthWord Press, Inc.
PO Box 1360
Minocqua, WI 54548

All rights reserved. No part of this work covered by the copyrights hereon may be reproduced or used in any form or by any means—graphic, electronic or mechanical, including photocopying, recording, taping of information on storage and retrieval systems—without the prior written permission of the publisher.

The copyright on each photograph in this book belongs to the photographer, and no reproductions of the photographic images contained herein may be made without the express permission of the photographer.

Editorial revisions and new text by Cathy D. Harrington
Index by Barbara Littlewood
Book design by Kenneth Hey
Maps by Todd Quamme

Front cover photograph: Foster Falls, Iron County; Back cover photograph: round-lobed hepatica.

Library of Congress Cataloging-in-Publication Data
The places we save : a guide to The Nature Conservancy's preserves in
     Wisconsin / by The Nature Conservancy of Wisconsin
               p.   cm.
          Includes index.
          ISBN 1-55971-597-9 (sc)
          1. Natural areas—Wisconsin—Guidebooks.   2. Wisconsin–Guidebooks.
     I. The Nature Conservancy (U.S.).   Wisconsin Chapter.
          QH76.5.W6P53   1997
          333.73'16'09775—DC21   96-46823

Printed in Merrill, Wisconsin, U.S.A.

The Places We Save

A Guide to The Nature Conservancy's Preserves in Wisconsin

The Nature Conservancy is a private, non-profit organization
dedicated to preserving plants, animals, and natural communities
that represent the diversity of life on Earth by protecting
the lands and waters they need to survive.

NORTHWORD PRESS, INC.
Minocqua, Wisconsin

Table of Contents

Pewit's Nest in the Baraboo Hills

Foreword
The Nature Conservancy in Wisconsin

Many of the people who have shaped our land values in the United States have been influenced in ways both big and small by the Wisconsin landscape. Not far from the Baraboo Hills, on the Wisconsin River, is the sand farm that inspired Aldo Leopold's seasonal sketches entitled *A Sand County Almanac.* It is also in Wisconsin where Leopold wrote his now-famous essay *The Land Ethic,* a powerful plea for humanity to see land as a community to which we all belong and to begin to use it with love and respect.

While John Muir is best known for his passionate writings about Yosemite and the mountains of California, he spent his youth on a farm near Portage, Wisconsin. In his book, *The Story of My Boyhood and Youth,* he recalls the happy days spent exploring the marshes and woodlands near his home. "Oh, that glorious Wisconsin wilderness!" he wrote. "Everything new and pure in the very prime of spring when Nature's pulses were beating highest and mysteriously keeping time with our own!"

It was in Sister Bay on the Door Peninsula that Sigurd Olson, the eloquent essayist and spokesman for the preservation of wilderness, wrote he believed he "heard the singing wilderness for the first time."

The beautiful and diverse landscapes that inspired these people have also inspired many generations of Wisconsin citizens to love, protect, and care for these lands. It is thanks to careful stewardship on their part that today the Conservancy is able to acquire and preserve places like the Baraboo Hills in Sauk and Columbia counties, Mink River Estuary in Door County, and Chiwaukee Prairie in Kenosha County.

This book is a guide to the places that The Nature Conservancy of Wisconsin and its members have saved. We invite you to visit these special places, to walk lightly therein, enjoying the color and fragrance of the wildflowers and the melodies of the songbirds. We encourage you to help us continue to protect these remaining wild places for future generations.

Kangaroo Lake in Door County

Why We Preserve the Diversity of Life

Virginia Rail

For more than forty-five years, The Nature Conservancy has focused on its mission—preserving the plants, animals, and natural communities that represent the diversity of life on Earth by protecting the lands and waters they need to survive. In essence, the Conservancy is committed to what Aldo Leopold called the "first precaution of intelligent tinkering." We have committed ourselves to "keeping every cog and wheel" for the benefit and enjoyment of future generations.

What are those cogs and wheels? They are natural communities such as tallgrass prairies, oak savannas, calcareous fens, boreal forests, and mixed hardwood forests. They are plant and animal species, such as the prairie white-fringed orchid, the Blanding's turtle, and the regal fritillary butterfly. They include all of the individual variation within these living organisms and the many interactions between them.

While there are many reasons for saving species and their habitat, self-interest seems to be the most compelling for many people. The natural world provides us with many of the medical, agricultural, and commercial products we use today. For example, 41 percent of the prescription medications dispensed in the United States contain chemicals derived from plants and animals. An extract from the rosy periwinkle, which grows in the tropics, is used to treat childhood leukemia. Millions of Americans with high blood pressure depend on regular doses of digoxin, which is obtained from a European species of foxglove. Taxol, a substance derived from Pacific yew, is being used in the treatment of certain types of cancer. It was a fungus that gave us penicillin.

Norman Myers, a consultant on environmental issues and resource economics at Oxford University, has estimated that societies around the world use about seven thousand kinds of plants for food but have come to depend on only about fifteen highly domesticated forms. The productivity of these fifteen major crops cannot be maintained, let alone expanded, without a constant infusion of fresh genetic variability. Much of this genetic material comes from wild plants, the relatives of modern crops. Wild plants also serve as sources of new crops that can eventually be cultivated and used by people.

Industry depends just as heavily on wild plants for raw materials as agriculture and medicine. Take the humble seaweeds, for example. These marine plants serve as a source of vitamin C, poultry meal, and meat and fish preservatives. They are used to grow bacteria, to keep toothpaste in the tube, to make ice cream smooth, to make puddings thick, and to help candy bars last longer. Many other plants are gathered by industry for their oils and fibers.

These are just a few examples of the many economic benefits that humans derive from the natural world. Many species of plants and animals have not even been discovered and named by scientists, let alone tapped for their economic potential.

While the economic benefits of conservation are important, there are also aesthetic reasons for saving species and natural communities. The beauty of nature lifts our hearts and inspires our minds. Who hasn't been inspired at least once by the beauty of a flower, a bird, or a lake to take the lens cap off a camera or dip a brush into paint and try to capture the moment forever? Nature has had a dominant influence on the arts since the first cave paintings. Nature is also our favorite place to recreate, be it hiking up a mountain, canoeing a rapid river, or strolling through a forest with binoculars ready for a fleeting glimpse of a brightly colored songbird.

We learn from the natural world. The forests, wetlands, and grasslands, the plants and animals that dwell therein, and all the many interactions between them are natural laboratories. Scientists conduct research there; teachers use them to train the scientists of tomorrow. There are numerous examples of how we learn from nature. Probably one of the most well known examples is the invention of the airplane. Orville and Wilbur Wright, like many before them, studied the wing structure and flight of birds to craft the first flying machine. A more recent example is the successful germination of a 1,288-year-old lotus seed from China by scientists at UCLA. They are hoping that their research will yield clues to the aging process in other organisms, including humans.

As the number of human inhabitants of our planet continues to grow and require more space and resources, our forests, wetlands, and prairies are increasingly being damaged or destroyed. These ecosystems and the species that comprise them provide many essential services such as pollination, soil production, breakdown of pollutants, and stabilization of hydrologic cycles; without these services our planet would cease to exist as we know it. Without intact, fully functioning ecosystems to use as models and as the source of living components, there is little chance that scientists will be able to rebuild or restore these damaged ecosystems.

Finally, there are ethical reasons for habitat conservation. Because humans are the dominant species on Earth, we have the power to preserve or destroy other living things and the habitat on which we all depend for survival. With this power comes responsibility. Aldo Leopold may have put it best in his essay *The Land Ethic*, when he said that "each individual is a member of a community of interdependent parts . . . . The land ethic simply enlarges the boundaries of the community to include soils, waters, plants, and animals, or collectively: the land." He goes on to say that this does not mean we shouldn't use these natural resources. But we should respect their right to continue to exist and, in some places, to continue to exist in their natural state.

For these reasons and many more, The Nature Conservancy is committed to the protection of ecosystems and the rich diversity of life that thrives therein. This is an ambitious goal and one that cannot be accomplished without the help of concerned citizens who are willing to take action to make habitat conservation a reality.

"One of the most exciting aspects of The Nature Conservancy's direct conservation approach is that one person can truly make a difference," states Peter McKeever, Director of the Wisconsin Chapter of the Conservancy. "One person with a dream of saving a special piece of land can often make it happen. And that's what this organization is about: Caring people doing something very tangible to make the Earth a better place for future generations."

Prairie white-fringed orchid

The Quiet Conservationists

The Nature Conservancy traces its roots to 1915 and the Ecological Society of America, a group of scientists concerned about the loss of natural areas. In 1927 the Society published *The Naturalist's Guide to the Americas*, which warned of the disappearance of natural areas, and began lobbying for their preservation. From this group sprang the Ecologists' Union, which was "devoted to the preservation of nature sanctuaries in all types of ecological communities of plants and animals." In 1950, the Union gave rise to The Nature Conservancy and began to call for a national system of natural area preserves. The Conservancy was incorporated in Washington, D.C. in 1951, beginning what is now one of the most active conservation organizations in the United States.

The mission of The Nature Conservancy is to preserve plants, animals, and natural communities that represent the diversity of life on Earth by protecting the lands and waters they need to survive.

The Nature Conservancy uses the best available conservation science to guide its work. We accomplish our mission using a three-pronged approach:

• identification of significant natural areas that harbor rare or endangered plant and animal species and natural communities;

• protection of those areas through purchase or other means (this includes assisting public and private conservation organizations in similar land acquisition efforts);

• stewardship and management of protected areas to ensure their long-term viability (this includes supporting research and education efforts on the needs of rare species and natural communities).

To date the Conservancy and its members have been responsible for the protection of more than 9 million acres in fifty states and Canada. It has helped like-minded partner organizations to preserve millions of acres in Latin America, the Caribbean, the Pacific, and Asia. While some Conservancy-acquired areas are transferred for management to other conservation groups, both public and private, the Conservancy owns and manages some 1,400 preserves—the largest private system of nature sanctuaries in the world.

Last Great Places: An Alliance for People and the Environment

For more than forty-five years, The Nature Conservancy's approach to conservation—acquiring land to protect habitat for rare species—has been extremely successful.

Volunteers at Mianus River Gorge, New York, TNC's first land protection project in 1955

Recently, however, the Conservancy has seen the need to broaden its work to include the protection of larger, ecosystem-wide landscapes. We saw our preserves being impacted, oftentimes negatively, by human activities taking place outside the preserves. The Conservancy decided that in order to ensure the long-term survival of the plants and animals on its preserves, new approaches would need to be developed and added to its traditional acquisition efforts.

In 1991, The Nature Conservancy formally launched its Last Great Places initiative. The goal was to save outstanding remaining ecosystems in the United States, Latin America, and the Pacific. The Conservancy continues to buy critical natural lands that harbor rare species. But it also works to encourage compatible human use of the lands and waters that surround these core natural areas.

The Conservancy recognizes the fact that people and nature share the large, ecologically rich areas of the planet. We are committed to working in partnership with local communities to preserve these Last Great Places in creative ways that enable people to continue to sustain themselves economically.

Some of the Conservancy's Last Great Places in Wisconsin include the Baraboo Hills in Sauk and Columbia counties, the Door Peninsula, and Lulu Lake in Walworth and Waukesha counties.

The Wisconsin Chapter is Born

The Wisconsin Chapter was born in the spring of 1960. Three members of the Wisconsin Academy of Sciences, Arts and Letters—Joe Hickey, Hugh Iltis, and Gene Roark—sent out a call to members to save some of Wisconsin's natural landscape and urged organization of a Nature Conservancy chapter in Wisconsin. Thirty-eight people attended the organizational meeting, and Paul Olson, then the principal of Midvale Elementary School, was elected president. For the next seventeen years, chapter business was conducted from Paul Olson's home where Conservancy volunteers would gather to fold and staple newsletters, lick stamps, and write thousands of addresses.

The first Wisconsin Chapter project was Abraham's Woods in Green County. This 40-acre woodland exhibits a rich understory of spring wildflowers and an intact over-story of maple, elm, and scattered oak, basswood, and other trees. Purchased in 1961, the preserve was transferred shortly thereafter to the University of Wisconsin and is now managed by the UW-Madison Arboretum.

Since 1960, the Wisconsin Chapter of The Nature Conservancy has protected more than 50,000 acres of prairie, wetland, and forest that harbor hundreds of rare plant and animal species. It manages 55 preserves located throughout the state, including Baxter's Hollow and Hemlock Draw in the Baraboo Hills, Chiwaukee Prairie and Lulu Lake in southeastern Wisconsin, and Mink River Estuary in Door County. Its membership has grown from 38 to more than 22,000 dedicated individuals. While the day-to-day operation of the Wisconsin Chapter is carried out by paid staff, more than 900 volunteers devote their time, talents, and energy to help the Conservancy accomplish its mission.

A Cooperative Approach to Conservation

The Nature Conservancy often joins forces with public and private conservation partners to secure protection of threatened natural areas. Together we can accomplish much more conservation than we could working individually. In some cases, partnership may mean that the Conservancy will acquire a significant natural area and transfer ownership, at cost or as a gift, to an appropriate steward such as a land trust, university, or local, state, or national public agency. Other times, partnership may involve the sharing of biological or land management information between the Conservancy and other groups.

Vegetation monitoring at Black Earth Prairie

In 1985, the Conservancy entered into a cooperative venture with the Wisconsin Department of Natural Resources (WDNR) to establish a Natural Heritage Inventory System. The Heritage System is an ongoing inventory of plants, animals, and natural communities that are threatened on a statewide or national basis. The Heritage staff of the WDNR Bureau of Endangered Resources gathers data on sites throughout the state and catalogs it in an integrated system of maps, computer databases, and paper files. The Nature Conservancy uses this information to identify the most significant natural areas in the state and set protection priorities. Heritage information is also available to land-use planners, land managers, and landowners to help them make good land-use, management, and protection decisions.

The Heritage System was developed by The Nature Conservancy in the 1970s out of a need to compare sites and elements of natural diversity so that protection efforts would be focused on the most threatened species and communities. Today there are Heritage programs in all fifty states and in other countries where the Conservancy is working.

Seed collecting at Spring Green

What Makes a Conservancy Preserve?

Nature Conservancy preserves come in all shapes and sizes. They may be as small as a three-acre sand prairie, which the Conservancy has acquired to protect an intact assemblage of prairie and sand barrens plants that is now almost extinct in Wisconsin. They may be as large as 3,300 acres of sandstone mesas, woods and wetlands in central Wisconsin where the Conservancy is preserving a bit of Wisconsin wilderness as it must have appeared to the first European settlers.

Sometimes preserves are part of larger-scale landscape projects, such as Baxter's Hollow in the Baraboo Hills. In the Hills, the Conservancy is working with local residents, landowners, business, and public and private agencies to protect an intact forested ecosystem that is unique in the Midwest.

What they all have in common is that they have been identified by the Conservancy, working with the Natural Heritage Program and other local scientific experts, as significant natural areas that are threatened and in urgent need of protection.

Protection can take many forms. Frequently, the Conservancy's first contact with a landowner is through the Natural Areas Registry Program. Registry is a voluntary commitment on the part of a landowner to protect the natural features on his or her property. The Conservancy also works with landowners to purchase land, accept gifts of land, and to negotiate conservation easements—legal agreements in which individuals retain ownership of their land but forfeit their right to use the land in ways that would destroy or damage the critical habitat.

Once natural areas have been protected, the Conservancy's commitment to stewardship kicks in. The role of Conservancy land managers or "stewards" is to manage irreplaceable natural lands so that their rare communities and species may flourish.

Key components of the Conservancy's stewardship program include: (1) commissioning and conducting research at preserves to determine the needs of species and communities; (2) providing for these needs; and (3) monitoring the results of land management efforts to ensure success.

Providing for the needs of a rare species or community may mean doing nothing, simply allowing natural processes to continue as they always have. But oftentimes, these natural processes have been disrupted, and active management is necessary. An example of this is a prairie, which is dependent on fire to maintain its health and diversity, but is no longer allowed to burn. In this situation, Conservancy stewardship staff and volunteers periodically conduct controlled burns that mimic the natural fires that once kept Wisconsin prairies free of invading shrubs.

Volunteers are crucial to the Conservancy's stewardship efforts. Besides helping with controlled burns, they also remove non-native plants, post boundaries, mend fences, tear down old buildings and other structures, and survey for rare plants and animals. They are an indispensable part of the Conservancy's stewardship team.

The Nature Conservancy of Wisconsin welcomes your support as a volunteer or as a financial contributor. Together we can protect the natural landscapes, plants and animals that make Wisconsin a great place to live for ourselves and for future generations.

State Natural Areas

Many Wisconsin Conservancy preserves are listed here as either a **Dedicated** or **Designated State Natural Area**. These are legal distinctions established by the Wisconsin State Legislature to extend environmental protection over areas of land or water that remain largely undisturbed and are of significant educational or scientific value. Dedication or Designation may apply to both private and public lands. The term Designated State Natural Area is used to protect land through an exchange of agreements between landowners and the State of Wisconsin. Designations may be canceled. Setting aside a Dedicated State Natural Area signifies a transfer of land or permanent conservation easement on the land to be held in trust for the people of Wisconsin. Dedication ensures protection of the land's natural values in perpetuity.

Guidelines for Visiting the Preserves

The Nature Conservancy's preserves are private properties, managed to protect native species and natural communities. Whenever a property is acquired through the support of members and friends, the Conservancy makes a commitment to protect the fragile characteristics of the preserve.

It would not be responsible to allow activities at preserves that could erode the very features the Conservancy has set out to protect. Consequently, some preserves, which harbor species or natural communities at risk, can only be visited for educational or research purposes with permission from Conservancy stewardship staff. Most Conservancy preserves, however, are open for careful public use as long as visitors enjoy these lands for passive recreation only—hiking, bird watching, nature study, and photography. Preserves that contain plants and animals of scientific interest are often used for biological and ecological research.

The Conservancy keeps trails and facilities to a minimum on its preserves. Our primary goal is to protect the unique natural features of the site. The trails we do maintain or create are designed to steer visitors away from the most fragile portions of the preserve and toward those that can tolerate more use.

Each preserve listing in this book includes details about visitor access. Those preserves that have limited access are listed as "Special Access Only." Contact the Conservancy office at 633 West Main Street, Madison, WI 53703 or call (608) 251-8140 for information about visiting these places for education or research purposes.

Make the most of your visit to a Conservancy preserve by observing these guidelines:

Come Prepared

Wear comfortable footwear suitable for hiking, but no heavy, cleated boots. Pack rain gear and wear long pants with socks over them to protect yourself from ticks and poison ivy or poison sumac. Bring along sunscreen and insect repellent for protection. For a long hike, outfit yourself with a filled water bottle for thirst quenching. And, of course, remember your camera, binoculars, compass, this guide, and other field guides to wildflowers, birds, butterflies, and other natural features.

Preserve Our Preserves

DO NOT pick flowers, berries, nuts, mushrooms, shells, rocks, or other parts of the natural landscape. Collecting plants, animals, and minerals is allowed for scientific research ONLY and requires a permit from the Wisconsin Conservancy office.

Dr. John Thomson leading a TNC field trip in the Baraboo Hills

Respect These Restrictions

The following activities are NOT ALLOWED on Conservancy preserves:

- Pets (even on a leash, except seeing-eye dogs);
- Horseback riding;
- Bicycles or other off-road vehicles;
- Camping or picnic fires;
- Rock climbing, rappelling, ice climbing, or spelunking;
- Fishing or trapping;
- Hunting (except by permit from Wisconsin office of The Nature Conservancy on preserves where deer damage is excessive).

Please do not trespass on private property adjacent to Conservancy preserves.

Enjoy your visit and please report any vandalism or other problems you encounter to the Conservancy. For more information about The Nature Conservancy and the Wisconsin Chapter, contact our office at 633 West Main Street, Madison, WI 53703, or call (608) 251-8140.

Wisconsin's Natural Landscape

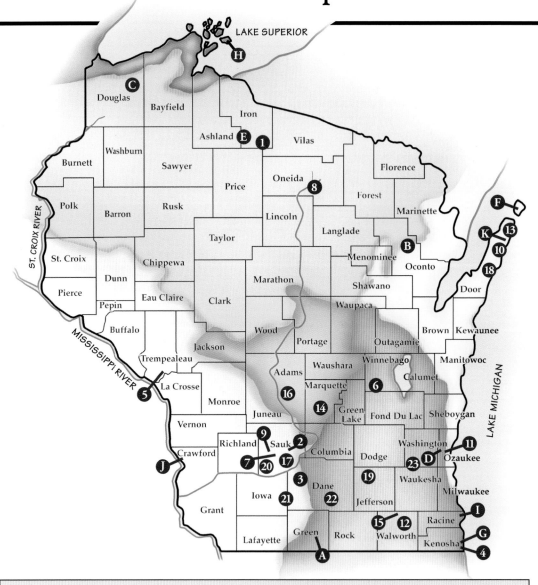

The State of Wisconsin can be divided into six natural regions, each one characterized by distinct geology, soils, vegetation, and habitats. It is a landscape of endless variety, from the pine forests and peat bogs of the Northern Highlands to the pure prairies of the Southeastern Moraines. The preserves described in this guide represent each of the six regional types defined here. All 34 sites described in the guide are marked on the map and organized into two sections: (1) preserves the Conservancy owns and manages; and (2) a sampling of preserves the Conservancy has played a role in protecting. Preserves appear in alphabetical order within each section. At the back of the book is a list of all sites the Conservancy has helped protect in Wisconsin (by county).

Preserves

1. Clifford F. Messinger Bass Lake Preserve
2. Baxter's Hollow/R.D. & Linda Peters Nature Preserve
3. Black Earth Rettenmund Prairie
4. Chiwaukee Prairie
5. Decorah Mounds
6. Owen & Anne Gromme Preserve
7. Hemlock Draw
8. Holmboe Conifer Forest
9. Honey Creek
10. Kangaroo Lake
11. Kurtz Woods
12. Lulu Lake Preserve
13. Mink River Estuary
14. Page Creek Marsh
15. Pickerel Lake Fen
16. Quincy Bluff & Wetlands
17. Schluckebier Sand Prairie
18. Shivering Sands
19. Snapper Memorial Prairie
20. Spring Green Preserve
21. Thomson Memorial Prairie
22. Waubesa Wetlands
23. Walter & Rose Zinn Preserve

Cooperative Projects

A. Abraham's Woods
B. Archibald Lake Hemlock Forest
C. Brule River
D. Cedarburg Bog
E. Flambeau River
F. Jackson Harbor Ridges
G. Kenosha Sand Dunes
H. Michigan Island
I. Renak-Polak Woods
J. Rush Creek Bluffs
K. Toft Point

▨ Lake Superior Boreal
- balsam fir and white spruce
- red clays and pink soils
- undulating to rolling plains
- peat extensive in some wetlands

▨ Northern Highlands
- maple, hemlock, and yellow birch interrupted by extensive stands of white and red (Norway) pines
- peat bog with black spruce, tamarack, and white cedar

▨ Western Driftless Upland
- hilly with little evidence of glaciation
- oak savanna, southern mesic forest
- pure prairie stands
- extensive river bottom forest

▨ Lake Michigan Lowland
- American beech range in Wisconsin
- southern and northern mesic forest interspersed with wetland
- maple, hemlock, yellow birch, and beech (northern)
- maple, basswood, elm, and beech (southern)

▨ Central Sands Transition
- nearly level terrain with sandstone buttes
- oak savanna and pine barrens
- vast wetland communities
- soils feature sand, shallow peats, and mucks

▨ Southeastern Moraines
- sequences of glaciated ridges and lowlands
- southern mesic forest, oak savanna
- pure prairie stands
- many wetland communities

Nature Conservancy Preserves

Mukwonago River, Lulu Lake Preserve

Baraboo Hills Region

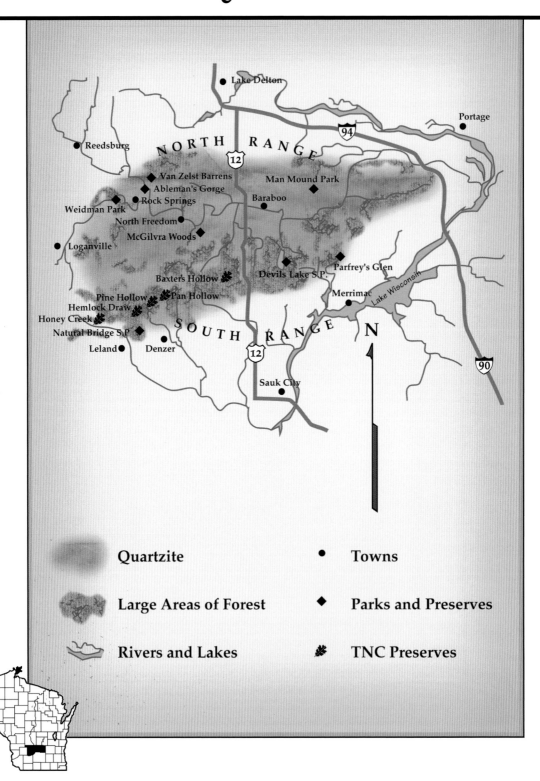

Lake Delton

Portage

NORTH RANGE

94

12

Reedsburg

◆ Van Zelst Barrens

◆ Ableman's Gorge
● Rock Springs

Man Mound Park ◆

Baraboo

◆ Weidman Park

North Freedom

McGilvra Woods ◆

Loganville

Baxter's Hollow ✿

Pine Hollow ✿ ✿ Pan Hollow

Hemlock Draw

Honey Creek ✿

Natural Bridge S.P. ◆

Leland ●   Denzer

12

Devils Lake S.P. ◆

Parfrey's Glen ◆

Merrimac   Lake Wisconsin

SOUTH RANGE   **N**

Sauk City

90

Legend

Quartzite   ● Towns

Large Areas of Forest   ◆ Parks and Preserves

Rivers and Lakes   ✿ TNC Preserves

Volunteer Harold Kruse leading a field trip in the Baraboo Hills

The Baraboo Hills of Sauk and Columbia counties are all that remain of one of the most ancient rock outcrops in North America. A forested sanctuary underlain by a durable rock called Baraboo quartzite, the Hills are an ecologically unique part of the Midwest. The extraordinary variety of plants and animals in the Baraboo Hills has prompted The Nature Conservancy to designate them a "Last Great Place." In taking this step, the Conservancy recognizes the Hills as one of the most important areas for biological diversity in the western hemisphere.

Long before the glaciers arrived, the ancient Baraboo mountain range dominated a landscape alternately covered by a vast inland sea or exposed to the forces of wind, rain, and the freezing and thawing action of weather. These forces and the sea gradually wore away the rose-colored quartzite, depositing some of the rubble in what is now Parfrey's Glen and other draws leading out of the Hills. After millions of years of erosion, the glaciers moved in, scraping the landscape with tremendous force. As recently as ten thousand years ago, glaciers moved across the eastern half of the Hills, leaving behind rock deposits that plugged a gap in the South Range and created Devils Lake.

Today the Baraboo Hills cover 144,000 acres within the Savanna Ecoregion, the area of the Midwest that lies between the deciduous forests to the east and the prairies of the west. The Savanna Ecoregion stretches over 40 million acres from north-central Minnesota into Indiana. The Baraboo Hills support 68 percent of the bird species found in this region and more than half of Wisconsin's native plants.

The oak, maple, and basswood forests of the Baraboo Hills constitute the largest block of upland forest still standing in southern Wisconsin. They provide habitat for more than 1,800 kinds of plants and animals and are a wellspring for life beyond the Baraboo Hills. For example, some forest songbirds, like the state-threatened acadian flycatcher, need large, unbroken tracts of forest in which to raise their young. In the Baraboo Hills, these birds can raise more young than the forest can hold; some of the birds move to woodlots outside the Hills, enriching places where they might not otherwise be found.

Punctuating the hilltops in the dense forests are oak and hickory glades that persist on soil that seemingly prohibits the growth of vigorous trees. In the glades' speckled sunlight, grow uncommon sun-loving plants, including prairie fame-flower, violet bush clover, and slender bush clover, a state-threatened species.

Through land acquisition and voluntary registry agreements, The Nature Conservancy has protected more than 6,000 acres in the Baraboo Hills at locations including Baxter's Hollow, Hemlock Draw, and Honey Creek (for more information, see individual entries). The Conservancy continues to work with private landowners, local communities, economic interests, and conservation partners to protect important natural habitats in the Baraboo Hills.

Baraboo Hills in winter

Clifford F. Messinger Bass Lake Preserve

Bass Lake

This preserve takes its name from a pristine 15-acre soft water lake, the first northern wilderness lake The Nature Conservancy has taken under protection. Bass Lake serves as the centerpiece for the deeply forested site, located in the Northern Highland natural region. This glaciated area contains the most extensive swamps and marshes (often called by their Chippewa name—*muskeg*) in the state.

Great diversity characterizes the vegetation at Bass Lake Preserve. Sugar maple, red maple, yellow birch, and white birch are there in a northern mesic forest type. The dry mesic forest is dominated by aspens and maples. In the swamp conifer forest rimming the lake and other water bodies, mature tamarack and black spruce trees grow along with large white pines. Virtually undisturbed bogs support additional shrubby vegetation such as the leatherleaf and bog laurel.

A wealth of shrubs and herbs make up the undergrowth throughout the preserve. Juneberry, alder-leaved buckthorn, raspberry and the American fly honeysuckle thrive here, along with pipewort, wild calla, sweet-scented bedstraw, sweet cicely, wild sarsaparilla, and the unusual pitcher plant.

Great horned owl

Clifford F. Messinger Bass Lake Preserve continued

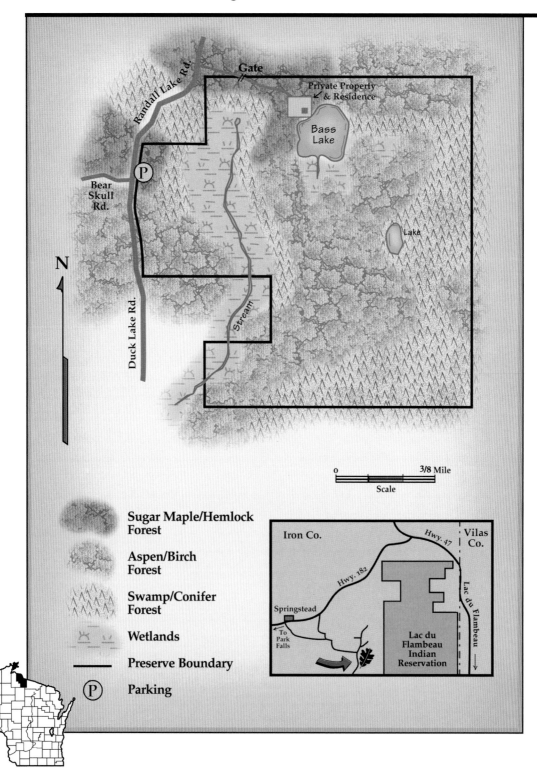

Gate

Randall Lake Rd.

Private Property & Residence

Bass Lake

P

Bear Skull Rd.

Duck Lake Rd.

Lake

Stream

N

0   3/8 Mile

Scale

Sugar Maple/Hemlock Forest

Aspen/Birch Forest

Swamp/Conifer Forest

Wetlands

Preserve Boundary

P   Parking

Iron Co.   Vilas Co.

Hwy. 47

Hwy. 182

Lac du Flambeau

Springstead

To Park Falls

Lac du Flambeau Indian Reservation

Water is a major theme at the preserve. In addition to Bass Lake, a short stream and a portion of a second lake, both unnamed, are part of the landscape. Wildlife, such as the great blue heron, osprey, and common loon, is found in abundance near these wetlands. Bald eagles and black bears have been spotted in the area, and beaver dams have been found along the length of the stream.

The size and quality of the Bass Lake project represent a significant ecological preserve that encompasses a complete northern Wisconsin lake watershed. Since the Conservancy acquired a conservation easement on the land in 1982, valuable scientific work has been conducted by the Wisconsin Department of Natural Resources and other groups.

In 1990, the Conservancy renamed the Bass Lake Preserve in honor of Clifford F. Messinger, former chair of The Nature Conservancy's national Board of Governors and of the Wisconsin Chapter Board of Trustees. Cliff Messinger donated all the land included in the preserve to The Nature Conservancy.

Protected: 840 acres. Northern Wisconsin. Located in Iron County, approximately 25 miles from Lac du Flambeau, Minocqua, Mercer, and Park Falls; west of Lac du Flambeau Indian Reservation. Dedicated as a State Natural Area. Owned and managed by The Nature Conservancy of Wisconsin.

Directions: From Park Falls, follow State Hwy 182 east approximately 20 miles to Bearskull Road; travel southeast approximately 4 miles to a "T" intersection with Randall Lake Road and Duck Lake Road. Park along east side of the road.

Visitor Access: Open year-round. No trails; uplands are accessible by foot but separated by large wetland areas. The two cabins and associated buildings on the shore of Bass Lake are still in private ownership; please respect the residents' privacy by not trespassing.

Baxter's Hollow/R.D. & Linda Peters Nature Preserve

Baxter's Hollow is one of the Wisconsin Chapter's most impressive projects. Since 1969, The Nature Conservancy has steadily acquired tracts of land here, making it the largest preserve in the Baraboo Hills today. Baxter's Hollow Preserve is remarkable for the large area of deep forest and the mountain-like creek that it protects. Despite years of human habitation, the land at Baxter's Hollow still seems wild and untouched.

The rich forest covering Baxter's Hollow is part of the state's largest intact southern deciduous forest. The forest is a mosaic of many parts. Thick stands of oak, hickory, maple, and ash grow on the quartzite bluffs that dominate the landscape. In the gorge that gives the preserve its name, yellow birch, white pine, maple, and basswood grow along the water's edge. Lightly forested openings, called acid bedrock glades, occur on the drier, more exposed rims of the bluffs. In spring a variety of wildflowers blossom in the forest of Baxter's Hollow, including Jacob's ladder and marsh marigold in low-lying spots; carpets of spring beauty, dogtooth violet, and hepatica on hillsides; and shooting stars and alum root in the glades.

Big Woods Thwart Nest Robbers

The populations of many forest songbirds such as the hooded warbler are shrinking. One cause of the decline is the brown-headed cowbird, an interloper from the Great Plains that moved east into Wisconsin and elsewhere following the widespread cutting of the forests. Unlike most birds, which build and tend their own nests, cowbirds lay their eggs in the nests of other birds. Since many of the nest parents cannot tell the difference between their own chicks and the cowbird chicks, they feed them both, but the fast-growing and demanding cowbird chicks take food away from the other chicks, which usually starve.

Cowbirds generally stay close to the edge of the forest and will not bother nests that are found deep in the woods. But forest cutting, road building, and residential development can open up the forest, making it possible for cowbirds to invade the nests of forest-interior songbirds. The big tracts of forest still found in the Baraboo Hills provide good homes for these forest-interior birds, but as the forest is divided into smaller and smaller tracts, the future for many forest songbirds grows dim.

Otter Creek, Baxter's Hollow

Otter Creek is the thread that ties the preserve together. It runs clear and fast over quartzite bedrock boulders, and its many small tributaries drain the largest undeveloped watershed in southern Wisconsin. The creek is home to a rich collection of aquatic life rare in Wisconsin, including the pickerel frog and at least five species of caddis flies found in few other places.

More than 40 species of birds breed in Baxter's Hollow. It is one of the most important nesting areas in southern Wisconsin for forest-dwelling birds. Birds that are rare in Wisconsin, such as the worm-eating warbler and the hooded warbler, occur at the preserve.

Private landowners in the Baraboo Hills have been important to the Conservancy's preservation efforts at Baxter's Hollow, making cooperative conservation of this critical bird and wildlife habitat possible.

The Nature Conservancy designated 220 acres in the heart of Baxter's Hollow as the R.D. & Linda Peters Nature Preserve in 1982. The R.D. & Linda Peters Foundation provided significant financial support to the Conservancy in the early 1980s for land acquisition at Baxter's Hollow.

Protected: 4,208 acres. Southwestern Wisconsin. Located in Sauk County between Sauk City and Baraboo. Dedicated as a State Natural Area. Owned and managed by The Nature Conservancy of Wisconsin.

Directions: Take US Hwy 12 northwest of Sauk City for 7.5 miles to intersection with Cty Hwy C, across from Badger Army Ammunition Plant. Turn west on Cty C and travel 1.5 miles to intersection with Stone's Pocket Road. Turn north and drive 2 miles into the woods and park at one of several turn-off parking sites, including one marked with a large preserve sign.

Visitor Access: Open year-round. Primitive, unmarked trail; very rocky conditions off-trail. Informational kiosk about 0.1 mile along trail into preserve. Some parcels of land within the preserve remain in private ownership and visitors are reminded not to trespass.

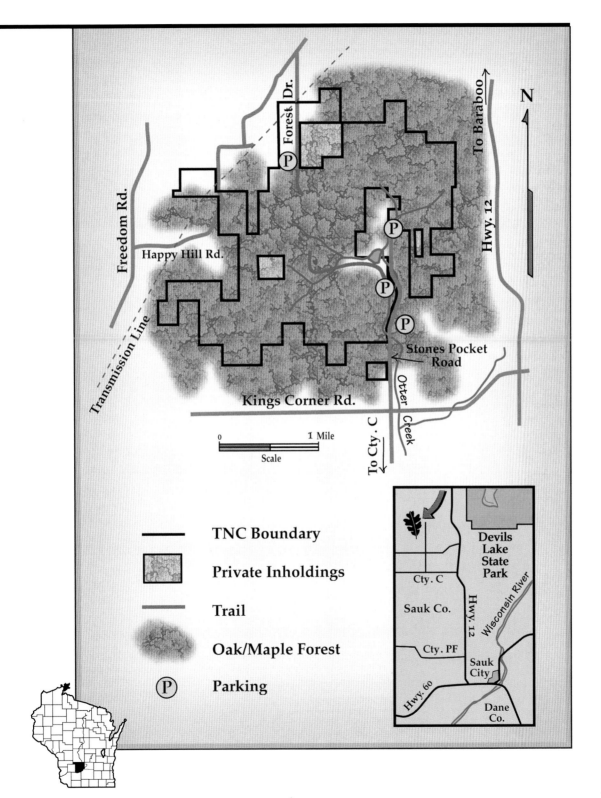

TNC Boundary

Private Inholdings

Trail

Oak/Maple Forest

Ⓟ Parking

Black Earth Rettenmund Prairie

B lack Earth Rettenmund Prairie is considered one of the best remaining examples of dry-mesic prairie in Wisconsin. This small, triangular tract of land, situated on the edge of a Dane County farm, sits on a low knob and ridge, clearly visible from the road. A wide diversity of plant species survive here. More than 80 have been identified, some of them on the State Endangered and Threatened Species list.

Among the rarest species existing at the Rettenmund Prairie is the round-stemmed false foxglove. Shrubs, aspen, and other young trees also grow along the ridge of the prairie, once rated among the top ten natural areas of Dane County in private ownership. After it was acquired by the Conservancy in 1986, Black Earth Rettenmund Prairie was dedicated as a State Natural Area, ensuring its continued protection.

Though there was some grazing on the land in the 1930s and evidence of a tractor path at one time, the prairie land has been preserved in recent years by brush removal and periodic burnings done by local volunteers. A strip of agricultural land on the northeast corner serves as a buffer from the roads that intersect there. Recordings of plant species began some years earlier when scientists from the University of Wisconsin conducted evaluations. The Rettenmund Prairie was once used by ecologist John Curtis for teaching, and today the area continues to be used as a natural laboratory of rare and abundant flora.

Protected: 16 acres. South-central Wisconsin. Located in Dane County, west of Black Earth. Dedicated as a State Natural Area. Owned and managed by The Nature Conservancy of Wisconsin.

Directions: Prairie lies in a triangle corner of a field southwest of the intersection of Fesenfeld Road and Cty Hwy F. From Black Earth, travel west on Cty Hwy KP (off State Hwy 78) for 1 mile, then south on Cty Hwy F for 0.25 mile to Fesenfeld Road and turn west. From Mazomanie, take Cty Hwy KP south 2 miles; turn west on Cty Hwy F and travel 0.25 mile to the Fesenfeld intersection. Park in the small parking lot off Fesenfeld Road at the west end of the preserve.

Visitor Access: Open year-round. No trails.

Butterfly weed and lead plant at Black Earth Prairie

Chiwaukee Prairie

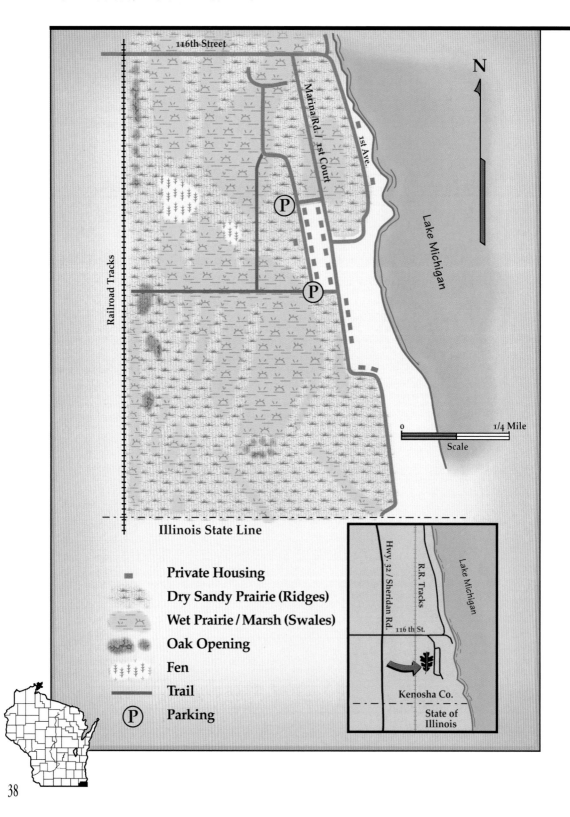

N

116th Street

Marina Rd. / 1st Court

1st Ave.

Lake Michigan

Railroad Tracks

P

P

0 — 1/4 Mile
Scale

Illinois State Line

Private Housing
Dry Sandy Prairie (Ridges)
Wet Prairie / Marsh (Swales)
Oak Opening
Fen
Trail
(P) **Parking**

Hwy. 32 / Sheridan Rd.

R.R. Tracks

Lake Michigan

116 th St.

Kenosha Co.

State of Illinois

It has been described as a "primeval sanctuary" left in the wake of the glacier that passed through Wisconsin and the upper Midwest some ten thousand years ago. Today, Chiwaukee Prairie is part of the last unbroken stretch of prairie of its kind in the state and is home to more than 400 plant species. Encompassing a narrow run of shoreline along Lake Michigan, about 4 miles south of Kenosha, Chiwaukee Prairie is a remnant of the past in the midst of urban and commercial development. Much of that development was arrested in 1965 when the Conservancy became involved in organized efforts to preserve this unique ecosystem. Chiwaukee Prairie is protected as a National Natural Landmark and a State Natural Area.

Chiwaukee Prairie is characterized as a "beach ridge complex," a landscape alternating between dry ridges and wet swales left in the lake's retreat. This combination of sand and clay soils gives Chiwaukee a rich and diverse vegetation that ranges from vast expanses of grassland, occasionally interrupted by small islands of open-grown oaks, to wet prairie plants in marshy shallows. The prairie provides habitat for several rare plants, including pink milkwort, smooth phlox, prairie Indian plantain, and sand coreopsis.

Each of the three growing seasons brings a different array of wildflowers into bloom at the prairie: shooting stars, prairie violets, and wood betony bloom in the spring; spiderwort, prairie phlox, and wild bergamot brighten the summer; acres of goldenrod, asters, and gentians in autumn. Mixed with the greens, golds, reds, and browns of big and little bluestem, Indian grass, and prairie dropseed, they make

Protected: 191 acres. Southeastern Wisconsin. Located in the Town of Pleasant Prairie in southeastern Kenosha County. Bordered on the south by the Wisconsin/Illinois state line, on the east by Lake Michigan. Dedicated as a State Natural Area. Owned and managed by The Nature Conservancy of Wisconsin and the University of Wisconsin-Parkside. The Wisconsin Department of Natural Resources Natural Areas Program manages an adjacent natural area to the north.

Directions: From I-94 between Kenosha and the Illinois state line, drive east on State Hwy 165 for about 6 miles. Turn south on State Hwy 32 (Sheridan Road) for 1 mile. Turn east on 116th Street (Tobin Road) for 1 mile. Turn south on 1st Court (Marina Road). Travel 5 blocks to 121st Street and turn west. Travel 1 block to Second Avenue and turn north. Continue to 119th Street.

Visitor Access: Open year-round. Informational kiosk at entrance to preserve. Self-guided trail to be completed Summer 1997; please stay on the trail to avoid trampling the prairie. Some parcels of land within the preserve remain in private ownership; please respect these landowners' property rights.

Chiwaukee one of the few places in Wisconsin where you can still walk for a mile amidst the fragrance, beauty, and stillness of a tallgrass prairie.

Chiwaukee Prairie is also home to a variety of wildlife. Red foxes, white-tailed deer, raccoons, thirteen-lined ground squirrels, and woodchucks roam the dry prairie ridges. Among some 76 bird species recorded, the upland sandpiper, king rail, marsh wren, and eastern meadowlark are protected at Chiwaukee. Numerous reptiles, amphibians and small mammals are found in abundance where lush prairie vegetation grades into swales—the shallow, wet prairie habitat that is an enduring feature of Chiwaukee.

Early Native American occupation of the site is apparent on the sand ridge to the west of Chiwaukee. There, chert flakes, scrapers, hunting points, and spears of Woodland and Upper Mississippi culture have been unearthed.

The name Chiwaukee was coined by developers in the 1920s who wanted to develop the area for luxury homes, a golf course, and a beachside hotel with train service from both Chicago and Milwaukee. These plans were abandoned during the Depression, but the land was subdivided and sold in small parcels to hundreds of individuals. Some homes and roads were built, but much of the land escaped development because it was low, wet, and unsuitable for development.

Preserving a Piece of Our Natural Heritage

Prairies, from the French word for meadow, are dramatic and beautiful landscapes that change with the seasons. Grasses are the dominant component of prairies: shorter species like Junegrass bloom in early summer and taller species such as big bluestem and Indian grass bloom later in August and September. Prairie wildflowers change with the seasons as well. Early bloomers like the pasque flower are succeeded by showy summer and fall species including butterfly weed, blazing star, and fringed gentians.

Wildfires once swept across these vast prairies and played an important role in maintaining them by returning nutrients to the soil, clearing off old growth, and preventing species not resistant to fire from moving in.

Prairies were once abundant in southern and western Wisconsin. Today, only about 2,000 of the 2.1 million acres of prairie once found in the state remain. The rest have been destroyed through conversion to agriculture, intense grazing, or development.

The Nature Conservancy has protected a number of prairie remnants. Visitors can still take a walk through a "sea of grass" at Thomson Prairie, Spring Green Prairie, Schluckebier Sand Prairie, and Chiwaukee Prairie.

Smooth phlox

Protection of Chiwaukee Prairie was initiated in 1965 by a dedicated group of local citizens who loved the prairie and wanted to preserve it for future generations. They contacted The Nature Conservancy for help with the funding they would need to acquire the more than 300 acres of remaining prairie. The local group began to track down the more than four hundred individual landowners who lived all over the country and abroad. In 1966, they made their first acquisition of a key parcel of land along the railroad corridor. Preservation of the prairie had begun.

Over the next thirty years, The Nature Conservancy acquired more than 350 lots at Chiwaukee Prairie. Some of the land has been transferred to UW-Parkside for scientific study and long-term protection and management. Local citizens continue to play a critical role in publicity, fundraising, and stewardship of the prairie.

Decorah Mounds

View from Decorah Mounds

Decorah Mounds is a classic Mississippi River bluff that provides a commanding view of the river valley and surrounding farmland. Mixed hardwood forest and dry prairie are combined here beneath the sweep of a vertical limestone cliff—1,200 feet above sea level at its highest point. The Nature Conservancy received Decorah Mounds as a gift from Harlan and Verneille Hunter, who farm the adjacent land. The first 30-acre parcel was donated in 1976 and an additional 10 contiguous acres added in 1986.

Decorah Mounds is in the driftless, or unglaciated, area of west-central Wisconsin where the land is characterized by greatly dissected uplands and lowlands covered with deep sediment from river flow. Though the predominant vegetation at Decorah is dry oak forest, the site is significant because of the high-quality dry prairie remnant at the top of the mound.

Prairie land once covered the entire south and east slopes. Now, Decorah Mounds is one of few such sites remaining in western Wisconsin, where most of the prairie has been lost to agriculture and forest. Since acquiring the preserve, the Conservancy has been working to restore this dry prairie from the small patch that existed in 1976. Overgrowth of sweet clover and aspen were threatening prairie plant species such as bluestem grasses, lead plant, puccoon, pasque flower, and butterfly weed. More frequent, controlled burning of overgrowth and dead grasses continues to help spark renewal of the Decorah prairie.

Purple prairie clover

43

Decorah Mounds continued

The forest at Decorah Mounds grades from large open-grown oaks with a dense understory of brush and blackberries to a more mesic, even-aged stand with ferns in the understory. Underbrush on the north slope is dominated by round-leaved dogwood and an abundance of young basswood. Shooting stars, trilliums, and Dutchman's-breeches have been found in the woods.

North of the prairie site, a vertical limestone cliff stands about ten feet high, composed of bare rock except for crevices where columbine and polypody ferns grow. White camas can be found at the top along the west boundary, its beauty matching the scenic vista from this point.

Wildlife thrives at Decorah Mounds. Animals sighted here include white-tailed deer, red fox, turkey vulture, rose-breasted grosbeak, red-bellied woodpecker, and indigo bunting.

Decorah Mounds' recorded history goes back more than a century and a half to the time when Winnebago Chief Decorah led a band of Indians against a threat from the Chippewa tribe. An old wagon road, built in the 1880s to connect the Decorah prairie to Galesville and points east, still defines one boundary of the site though the road was abandoned some ninety years ago. The east slope was logged prior to 1925 and the north mound logged in the late 1930s and 1940s. The entire area was used as grazing land until about 1950.

Previous owner Harlan Hunter grew up on this land and wanted to see it protected. When he and his wife gave the land to the Conservancy, they maintained their personal interest in Decorah Mounds by serving on the local committee that watches over the site, continuing to welcome visitors and answer their questions.

Protected: 40 acres. West-central Wisconsin. Located 2 miles east of Galesville in Trempealeau County. River bluff and prairie opening are along the western edge of Harlan Hunter's farm. Owned and managed by The Nature Conservancy of Wisconsin.

Directions: Travel southeast from Galesville on Hwy 53/35/54 about 2.25 miles to State Hwy 54; go north on Hwy 54 for 0.5 mile to a sharp corner where road heads east; park in or just off driveway of Harlan Hunter, fire number W17586. Walk west along edge of field 0.25 mile to southeast corner of preserve.

Visitor Access: Open year-round. No trails; can reach the mound by hiking up steep wooded slopes. Poison ivy is abundant.

Red fox

Owen & Anne Gromme Preserve

T he lakeshore, sedge meadows, and uplands of Rush Lake have inspired many scenes painted by noted Wisconsin wildlife artist Owen Gromme. It is fitting, then, to recognize the Gromme conservation tradition through this ambitious project.

Rush Lake, a 3,200-acre shallow, marshy lake, emerged from the most recent glaciation some twelve thousand years ago. The broad, shallow lake basin and widely varying drainage patterns indicate the influence of the glacier. The water levels at Rush Lake fluctuate under natural conditions. These changing water levels, combined with sedge meadows, prairie, and oak openings in the uplands, create an ideal environment for wildlife.

Two hundred years ago, a visitor to Rush Lake would have seen bison, elk, gray wolves, and black bears roaming the uplands. The booming of greater prairie-chickens in the spring, along with upland sandpipers, sharp-tailed sparrows, Le Conte's sparrows, and Henslow's sparrows, made the meadows and oak openings come alive. The marsh itself abounded with nesting populations of waterfowl.

Today, the visitor sees scattered remnants of oak savanna, prairie, and sedge meadows on the uplands. Because the shores of the lake are predominantly marshland, there is little shoreline development. The Rush Lake area is most significant for its outstanding migratory and breeding bird populations. The lands provide habitat for many species of waterfowl, including one of the state's largest populations of red-necked grebe, which is threatened in Wisconsin, and Forster's tern, a state-endangered species. In addition, the Rush Lake area is recognized by Wisconsin's sportsmen for its game species.

The Nature Conservancy made its first acquisition at Rush Lake in 1988. Today, the Conservancy owns and manages 608 acres at the Owen & Anne Gromme Preserve. The Conservancy is working cooperatively with private landowners, other conservation organizations, the U.S. Fish and Wildlife Service, and the State of Wisconsin to secure long-term protection for the highest quality natural communities and endangered species habitat in the Rush Lake watershed. In this way, The Nature Conservancy has the opportunity to protect and manage part of Wisconsin's original landscape.

Oak savanna

Long Distance Travelers

Every year between two and five billion birds migrate across America to the tropics and back again. On these journeys birds face numerous dangers, including starvation in the event of an early frost, getting blown off course and, for smaller birds, heavy predation. Wisconsin's prairies, wetlands, and forests provide important habitat for migratory birds, both as breeding and nesting grounds in spring and summer and as stopping points during migration. Preserving this link in the annual migration routes of many birds is vital to maintaining their populations.

As important as preserving summer grounds for migratory birds is maintaining their winter habitat in the tropics. To this end, the Wisconsin Chapter is committed to preserving 2 million acres of rain forest in Nicaragua, known as the BOSAWAS Reserve. This rain forest provides wintering habitat for migratory birds as well as a home for native species including jaguars, howler monkeys, and canopy orchids. To learn more about the Conservancy's work in Nicaragua, call our Communications Coordinator at (608) 251-8140.

Protected: 608 acres. South-central Wisconsin. Located north of Ripon in Winnebago and Fond du Lac counties. Dedicated as a State Natural Area. Owned and managed by The Nature Conservancy.

Directions: To reach preserve land on west side of lake, take State Hwy 44 north from its intersection with State Hwy 23 in downtown Ripon. Go about 0.25 mile to where Hwy 44 splits and take Cty Hwy E. Follow Cty E approximately 3.5 miles and watch for dirt road to preserve on east side of road, across from a house with fire number 689. Look closely to find the Conservancy signs at the entrance.

Additional accessible Conservancy lands are also located on the southeastern and eastern sides of the lake. From Ripon follow Cty Hwy E to the north approximately 2 miles to the intersection with Cork Street and turn east. Follow Cork Street for 2.25 miles to a "T" intersection with Island Road. Turn north and travel 1.5 miles. Turn west on Radtke Road. Parking is available almost immediately on the north side; look for flattened area where gravel has been removed.

To reach a third Conservancy area, go back on Island Road (south) 0.25 mile to Sportsman Road and turn east. Follow Sportsman Road 3 miles (it will take a sharp turn after 1.5 miles) to a "T" intersection with Mountain Road. Turn west and travel 0.5 mile. Mountain Road turns north and becomes Sportsman Road again. Preserve land is located on either side of the road. Park on shoulder out of way of traffic.

Visitor Access: Open year-round. No trails. Wetlands are abundant. Hike with care during the fall duck hunting season.

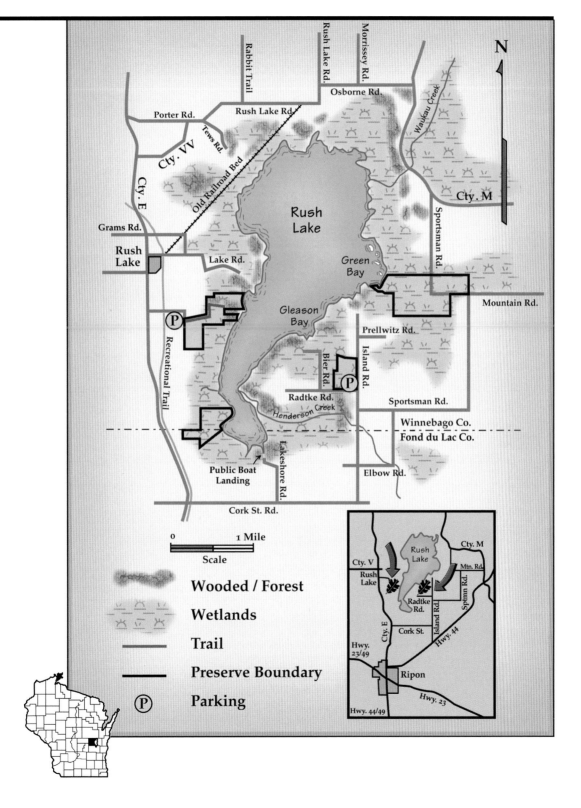

N

Rabbit Trail

Rush Lake Rd.

Morrissey Rd.

Osborne Rd.

Waukau Creek

Porter Rd.

Rush Lake Rd.

Tews Rd.

Cty. VV

Cty. E

Old Railroad Bed

Cty. M

Grams Rd.

Rush Lake

Lake Rd.

Rush Lake

Green Bay

Sportsman Rd.

Gleason Bay

Mountain Rd.

Prellwitz Rd.

Bier Rd.

Island Rd.

Recreational Trail

Radtke Rd.

Sportsman Rd.

Henderson Creek

Winnebago Co.
Fond du Lac Co.

Public Boat Landing

Lakeshore Rd.

Elbow Rd.

Cork St. Rd.

0   1 Mile
Scale

Wooded / Forest

Wetlands

⸺ **Trail**

▬ **Preserve Boundary**

ⓟ **Parking**

Inset map:

Cty. V

Rush Lake

Cty. M

Mtn. Rd.

Rush Lake

Spring Rd.

Cty. E

Radtke Rd.

Cork St.

Island Rd.

Hwy. 44

Hwy. 23/49

Ripon

Hwy. 44/49

Hwy. 23

Hemlock Draw

Hemlock Draw in the Baraboo Hills

Hemlock Draw represents one of the Wisconsin Nature Conservancy's greatest moments. It is among the Chapter's earliest acquisitions in the Baraboo Hills, first purchased in 1964 and conceived as a forest study area. It is now a major preserve in the Hills. The preserve has grown during nearly two decades of land purchase and donation and now includes a rocky canyon with clear-flowing stream, abundant woods, and an area of abandoned fields returning to native plant life. Hemlock Draw shelters several rare plants, including drooping sedge and, on the cliff, kidney-leaved sullivantia. The worm-eating warbler is one of several rare birds found here.

The plant communities at Hemlock Draw include five major kinds of forest and several interesting cliff and glade communities. Dense stands of hemlock line the stream and shelter many northern forest plants such as several species of club-mosses. Sedges, skunk cabbage, and witch hazel also grow along the flat-bottomed draw. On the flanks of the draw, hemlock and other northern species give way to rich forests of sugar maple, red oak, ironwood, and bigtooth aspen. Wood anemone, wild geranium, and early meadow rue all flower abundantly under the large trees. Drier forests dominated by red oak grow on the bluff tops north and south of the draw.

Hemlock Draw shelters many northern forest plants

Hemlock Draw continued

The fact that this area was not recently glaciated may hold the key to the diversity of life in the draw, where plant and bird species with affinities to northern areas of the state grow near the typical plants and animals of southern Wisconsin. The northern species may be relics from the time when the edge of a towering ice mass was a few miles to the east. They are able to persist at Hemlock Draw today because the narrowness of the draw maintains cool and moist conditions similar to the climate found farther north.

Another interesting aspect of Hemlock Draw is its geology. Formations of sedimentary rock exposed within the preserve furnish evidence that the Baraboo Hills were a chain of sea islands in the Cambrian-Ordovician periods, some 500 million years ago. The sandstone deposits formed during this era lie above the much older Baraboo quartzite, which is revealed in one of the finest geologic features of the preserve, a narrow pillar of rock called a "sea stack." The sea stack is a reminder of the time when tempestuous storms stirred an ancient island sea, eroding the quartzite bedrock and creating formations like those now found along rocky coastlines on the edges of this continent.

Hemlock Draw provides important habitat for wildlife. More than 40 species of breeding birds, including barred owls, ruffed grouse, wood thrush, black-capped chickadee, 6 species of warblers and 4 species of woodpeckers, depend on Hemlock Draw for food and cover.

Protected: 543 acres. Southwestern Wisconsin. Located in Sauk County near Leland. Owned and managed by The Nature Conservancy of Wisconsin.

Directions: Take US Hwy 12 northwest of Sauk City for 2.5 miles to the intersection with Cty Hwy PF; turn west on Cty PF and travel for 12 miles to County Hwy C; turn north on Cty C into Leland (0.25 mile); in Leland, turn north on Hemlock Road and travel 2 miles to Reich Drive; travel north on Reich Drive for approximately 0.5 mile to reach the preserve gate. When parking, do not block Reich Drive; local farmers move large equipment on the road. Park on the shoulder of the road south of the mailbox. North Entrance: Visitors can enter Hemlock Draw from Buck Fever Road at the north end of the preserve. However, please be aware that Buck Fever Road is very rough and steep. It is recommended that visitors entering from the north park on the shoulder of Schara Road and walk in.

Visitor Access: Open year-round. Primitive, unmarked trail.

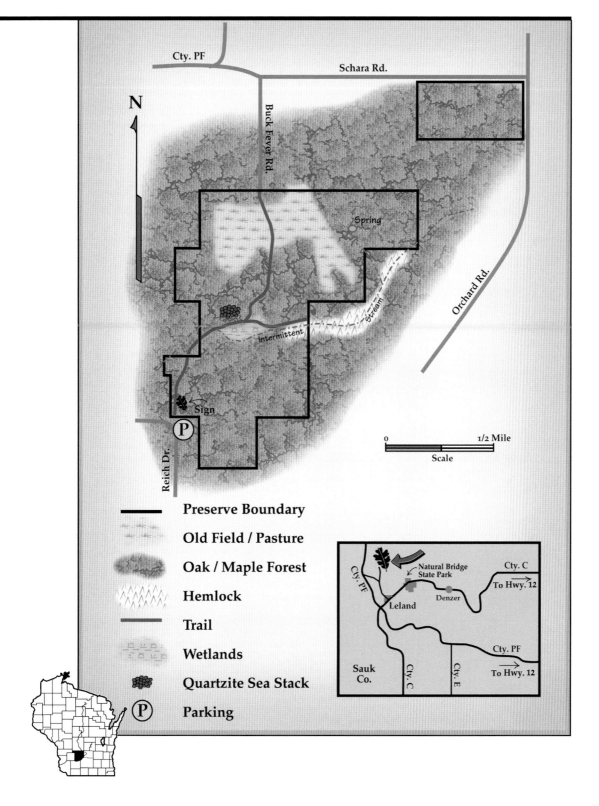

N

Cty. PF

Schara Rd.

Buck Fever Rd.

Spring

Orchard Rd.

Intermittent Stream

Sign

(P)

Reich Dr.

0   1/2 Mile

Scale

Preserve Boundary

Old Field / Pasture

Oak / Maple Forest

Hemlock

Trail

Wetlands

Quartzite Sea Stack

(P) **Parking**

Cty. PF

Natural Bridge
State Park

Cty. C

To Hwy. 12

Leland

Denzer

Cty. PF

To Hwy. 12

Sauk
Co.

Cty. C

Cty. E

Holmboe Conifer Forest

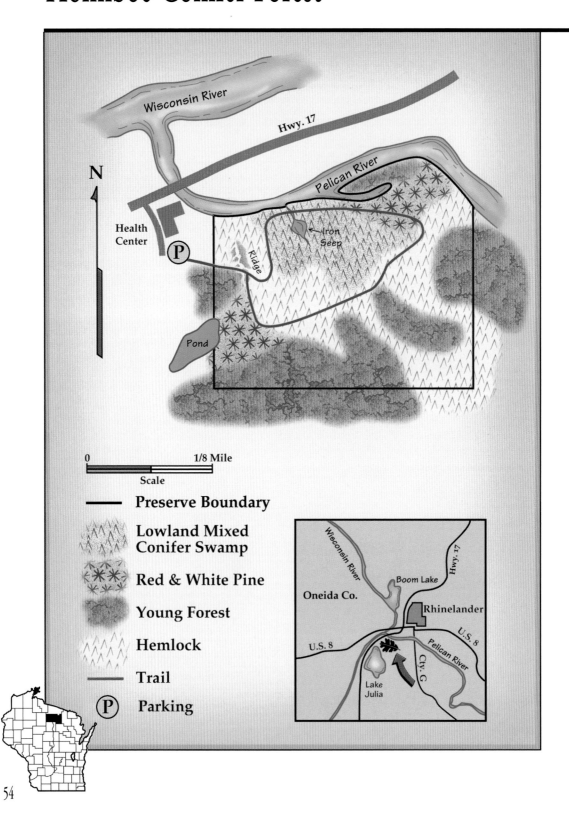

Wisconsin River

Hwy. 17

Pelican River

N

Health Center

P

Ridge

Iron Seep

Pond

0   1/8 Mile

Scale

— Preserve Boundary

Lowland Mixed Conifer Swamp

Red & White Pine

Young Forest

Hemlock

— Trail

P Parking

Wisconsin River

Oneida Co.

Boom Lake

Hwy. 17

Rhinelander

U.S. 8

U.S. 8

Pelican River

Cty. G

Lake Julia

It is a familiar picture to anyone who has traveled the rural roads of northern Wisconsin—majestic pine trees growing alongside maple, aspen, and birch. Underneath runs a network of upriver streams and tributaries that feed the Wisconsin River. The forest floor is a cool greenhouse of sedges and forest marsh plants. Holmboe Conifer Forest is the essence of such a natural woodland, able to support a wide range of tree species, ground cover, and soil types. The peace of nature abides here where more than 23 bird species find refuge.

The predominant features of the Holmboe Preserve are the rolling contours of swamp and uplands, punctuated by the glacial esker, or gravel ridge, that runs along the western boundary. The soil mix of alluvium or river sediment, marsh, loam, and sand supports a rich ecosystem, most notably the trees of Holmboe. White and red pines grow on the south ridges. In the swamps between ridges, tamarack and white cedar in isolated stands have taken hold. Swamp hardwoods at Holmboe include yellow birch, black ash, and alder. On the northern slopes, hemlock and fir abound and on the west side, where gravel diggings were once done, trembling aspens grow. The yew, one of the rarest of trees in Wisconsin, is found at Holmboe. Good stands are often lost to deer browsing in the area.

Along the forest floor, princess pine, three species of ground pine, barren strawberry, Pennsylvania sedge, labrador tea, pink lady's-slipper, and many other lowland species are present. Seeping springs on the preserve drain into the Pelican River and provide the necessary moisture for the cedar vegetation of Holmboe and adjacent land.

Protected: 32 acres. Northern Wisconsin. Located in Oneida County near Rhinelander, on the south bank of the Pelican River. Designated a State Natural Area. Owned and managed by The Nature Conservancy of Wisconsin.

Directions: Travel south on State Hwy 17 out of Rhinelander. Immediately after crossing the Pelican River, look for the Taylor Park Health Care facility on south side of river. Pull in driveway to back parking lot. Walk east about 50 yards across grassy area toward woods. Follow path to the kiosk and into preserve.

Visitor Access: Open year-round. Informational kiosk at entrance to preserve. Well-defined, marked, loop trail. Boardwalks over most wet areas.

Holmboe Conifer Forest continued

Pelican River, Holmboe Conifer Forest

The Holmboe Conifer Forest has been designated a Wildlife Sanctuary, a fact that ensures no disturbance and makes it possible for a sizable bird community to thrive. Species observed include the green-backed heron, spotted sandpiper, least flycatcher, eastern wood-pewee, purple martin, hermit thrush, veery, and the red-eyed vireo.

The Holmboe Conifer Forest was donated to the Conservancy by Frithjof Holmboe and his son, Thorvald. The Conservancy assumed full ownership and management of the preserve in 1965. Except for foot trails, there has been little disturbance to the land since logging days in the early part of the century. Remains of shanties were found along the ridge near the river where there was said to be a "hobo jungle" during the 1930s. The Holmboe Preserve was designated a State Natural Area in 1969 and is often used for educational purposes.

Princess pine

Honey Creek

Honey Creek Valley lies at the southwestern corner of the Baraboo Hills amid upland forests and wetlands that support numerous rare plant communities and more than 150 bird species. The best examples of several lowland communities in the Baraboo Hills are found at Honey Creek. In cooperation with the Wisconsin Society for Ornithology (WSO), The Nature Conservancy is working to protect this important area in the Baraboo Hills.

A stream gorge woven through part of an extinct glacial lake bed at the northern end of Honey Creek harbors diverse upland and lowland communities. In the uplands, red oak and sugar maple forests support nesting populations of rare forest birds such as the cerulean and Kentucky warblers. In spring, the forest floor is carpeted with bloodroot, hepatica, Dutchman's breeches, and other wildflowers. Turkey vultures often can be seen riding the air currents over the bluffs and likely nest in the preserve's rocky gorge. On shaded sandstone cliffs, small hemlock groves support numerous bird species, including black-and-white warblers.

In the lowlands, pockets of wet forest dominated by black ash, American elm, and tamarack, scattered white pines, and speckled alder thickets are interspersed with sedge meadows and cattail marshes; uncommon plants include bog bluegrass. A trout stream

Wisconsin Society for Ornithology

The Wisconsin Society for Ornithology (WSO) was founded in 1939 "to encourage the study of Wisconsin birds." Members in the group range from professional ornithologists to those who enjoy bird watching; they hail from many other states and countries around the world. Since WSO's founding, its goals have expanded to include the enjoyment of birds, bird habitat preservation, management research, and alerting members and the public to threats to Wisconsin's bird populations. WSO's quarterly publication, *The Passenger Pigeon*, keeps members updated on planned events, provides extensive lists of birds sighted throughout the state, and reports on bird-related research. In 1958, WSO began acquiring bog and woodland habitat at Honey Creek in the Baraboo Hills. Today the Honey Creek Natural Area encompasses 300 acres and includes trails and a permanent Nature Center.

To join WSO or receive additional information, contact: Wisconsin Society for Ornithology, Alex Kailing—Membership Chairman, W330 N2875 W. Shore Dr., Hartland, WI 53029-9732.

Cape May warbler

Honey Creek continued

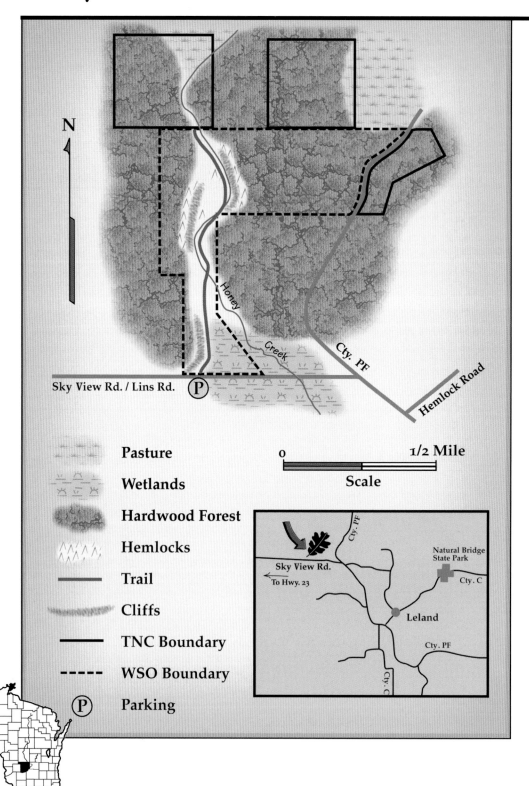

N

Honey

Creek

Sky View Rd. / Lins Rd. Ⓟ

Cty. PF

Hemlock Road

Pasture

Wetlands

Hardwood Forest

Hemlocks

Trail

Cliffs

TNC Boundary

WSO Boundary

Ⓟ Parking

0   1/2 Mile
Scale

Cty. PF

Sky View Rd.
To Hwy. 23

Natural Bridge
State Park

Cty. C

Leland

Cty. PF

Cty. C

running through the wet forest supports American brook lamprey and various darters and minnows. The rare pickerel frog also survives at Honey Creek.

The marshes and backwaters provide habitat for scores of birds including marsh wren, wood duck, blue-winged teal, great blue heron, green-backed heron, American woodcock, common snipe, veery, sora, Virginia rail, swamp sparrow, yellow-throated vireo, and Louisiana waterthrush.

During migration, large numbers of tree swallows congregate in these lowlands. The southerly exposure of the valley and abundance of insects attract acadian, least, and great crested flycatchers, eastern wood-pewees, eastern kingbirds, blue-gray gnatcatchers, and a variety of warblers.

It was the abundance of birdlife concentrated in this 2.5-mile-long valley that prompted the Wisconsin Society for Ornithology to begin buying land at Honey Creek in 1958 to establish a nature preserve. Today WSO owns and manages 300 acres at the Honey Creek Natural Area. The Conservancy acquired its first 28 acres at Honey Creek in 1969. Since that time, the two organizations have worked cooperatively to manage the land and host field trips and work parties at Honey Creek. The Nature Conservancy has also helped private landowners at Honey Creek voluntarily protect their land through the Natural Areas Registry Program.

Protected: 478 acres (TNC) and 300 acres (WSO). Southwestern Wisconsin. Located in Sauk County northwest of Leland. Owned and managed by The Nature Conservancy of Wisconsin and the Wisconsin Society for Ornithology.

Directions: Take US Hwy 12 northwest of Sauk City for 2.5 miles to the intersection with Cty PF; turn west on Cty PF and travel for 14 miles to the intersection with Sky View Road (formerly known as Lins Road). Turn west on to Sky View Road and travel 0.33 mile. The WSO trailhead is located on the north side of Sky View Road. Parking is available for a few vehicles along the roadside.

Visitor Access: Open year-round. Primitive, unmarked trail; hiking can often be over wet ground.

Kangaroo Lake

Kangaroo Lake

The mosaic of upland forests with dolomite outcrops, lowland forests, marshes, and a stream surrounding the north end of Kangaroo Lake constitutes a rich and diverse landscape. Long appreciated by Door County residents for its aesthetic values, it is now being protected by local conservation organizations and The Nature Conservancy for its biological richness as well.

A causeway built before the turn of the century separates the southern highly developed portion of the lake from the north end, which has almost completely escaped development. This lack of development is due largely to the extensive shoreline marshes and surrounding lowland forests.

Kangaroo Lake is a shallow, marl-bottomed basin with calcium-rich water. Marl is a mixture of silt, clay, and calcium carbonate. The calcium carbonate precipitates out of calcium-enriched waters as a result of the respiration of aquatic plants. Large, shallow marl lakes, while common to Door County, are uncommon regionally. Those that have escaped intensive shoreline development are especially rare.

Originating in an unusual marl fen about 5 miles north of Kangaroo Lake, Piel Creek flows into the lake from the northwest through a large lowland white cedar/black ash forest. Springs that probably feed Piel Creek throughout its length are visible at the point where the creek enters the lake. Piel Creek is one of less than fifteen sites in the world where the federally endangered Hine's emerald dragonfly has been found.

The landscape around the north end of Kangaroo Lake is generally low with the noted exception of the dolomite plateau west of the lake, which rises 110 feet above the lake surface. This plateau has a high concentration of bedrock crevices and fractures as well as numerous areas of exposed bedrock. The forest on this plateau is dominated by sugar maple, beech, white birch, and red oak and has a rich display of spring wildflowers.

White cedar and black ash, with lesser numbers of tamarack, black spruce, and balsam fir, dominate the large lowland forest at the north end of the lake. Shrubs such as speckled alder, willows, meadow sweet and dogwood populate the understory of the forest. Typical understory plants here include goldthread, naked miterwort, dewberry, and starflower. Canada yew, a regionally declining species, is abundant on a small peninsula that juts out into the north basin of the lake from the southeast shore.

In addition to the Hine's emerald dragonfly, the Kangaroo Lake/Piel Creek area provides habitat for several other rare species including the dorcas copper butterfly, bald eagle, osprey and Caspian tern. Black terns nest in the marshes. The marshes at the north end of the lake are also important breeding and migrational staging sites for sandhill cranes, Canada geese and other waterfowl. During the breeding season, blue-winged and golden-winged warblers have been seen in an old beaver meadow about a mile north of Kangaroo Lake.

Rare Green-eyed Dragon in Door County

Dragonflies are one of the most spectacular and colorful groups of insects. They are also excellent fliers and use this skill to catch mosquitoes, biting flies, and gnats. One of the most endangered species of dragonfly in the United States is the Hine's emerald dragonfly. There are only two known areas, one in Illinois and the other in Door County, that support breeding populations. Also known as Hine's bog skimmer and Ohio emerald dragonfly, the Hine's emerald gets its name from its bright emerald-green eyes and metallic green body. A fairly large insect at 2.5 inches long with a 3.3-inch wingspan, it inhabits calcareous (high in calcium carbonate) marshes. These wetlands are frequently found overlying dolomite bedrock. Like all wetlands, these areas are easily destroyed, and the disappearance of the Hine's emerald dragonfly from sites in Ohio seems to suggest that habitat destruction is the biggest threat to its existence. In light of its rarity and susceptibility to habitat destruction, it is currently listed as a federally endangered species.

Kangaroo Lake continued

In 1995 the Conservancy acquired 117 acres at the north end of Kangaroo Lake. The Conservancy is working with two local conservation organizations, the Door County Land Trustees and the Kangaroo Lake Association, to protect the north basin. The Conservancy transferred 57 acres of the property to the Door County Land Trustees for long-term protection and management in 1996.

Protected: 117 acres. Northeastern Wisconsin. Located southwest of Bailey's Harbor in Door County. Owned by The Nature Conservancy (60 acres) and the Door County Land Trustees (57 acres).

Directions: From Bailey's Harbor, travel south on State Hwy 57 approximately 1 mile to Cty Hwy E. Canoe Access: Travel west on Cty E for about 1 mile until you reach the causeway between the north and south ends of Kangaroo Lake. Park on the north side of the road at the east end of the causeway. Site is on the west side of the lake at the mouth of Piel Creek. Hiking Access: Travel west on Cty Hwy E for 2 miles to the stop sign at the intersection of Cty E and Logerquist Road. Turn north at the stop sign, staying on Cty E. The trail into the preserve is about 0.25 mile north on Cty E on the east side of the road. Park along the side of the road.

Visitor Access: Open year-round. Wetlands best viewed from canoe. Primitive, unmarked trails. Watch for snowmobiles on main trail in winter.

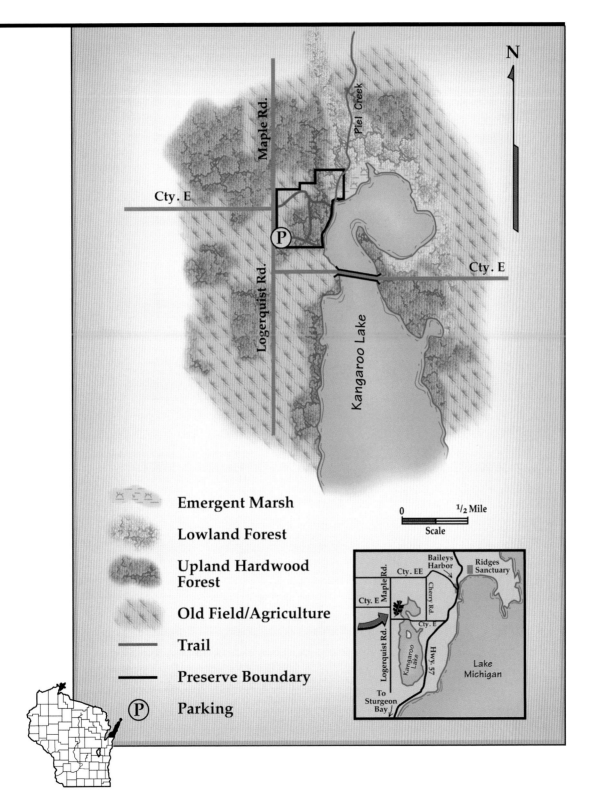

Emergent Marsh

Lowland Forest

Upland Hardwood
Forest

Old Field/Agriculture

Trail

Preserve Boundary

P   Parking

Maple Rd.

Cty. E

Piel Creek

N

Logerquist Rd.

Cty. E

Kangaroo Lake

0   ½ Mile
Scale

Baileys
Harbor

Cty. EE

Ridges
Sanctuary

Maple Rd.

Cherry Rd.

Cty. E

Cty. E

Logerquist Rd.

Kangaroo
Lake

Hwy. 57

Lake
Michigan

To
Sturgeon
Bay

Kurtz Woods

Bloodroot

Few remnants remain of the deep forests that characterized the presettlement era in southeastern Wisconsin. Kurtz Woods is one of them, all the more valuable because it is a relatively undisturbed southern mesic forest that hosts more than 82 species of trees and spring ephemerals.

The forest is dominated by sugar maple and American beech. White ash, basswood, and black cherry constitute a younger set of trees that spread east and west from the center of the preserve. The appearance of pole-size trees along the southeast boundary, evidence of logging in the 1930s, and an old granite quarry along the southwest edge are the only reminders of earlier land use and the last signs of disturbance here.

An assortment of spring wildflowers shares the forest floor with shrubs and young trees. These include hepatica, bloodroot, wild leek, and the aptly named spring beauty. Kurtz Woods is designated as a State Natural Area because of this diversity and the quality of the intact forest.

The terrain of Kurtz Woods is the lightly rolling, sandy moraine of the Lake Michigan Coastal Zone. Kettle depressions and glacial boulders can be seen throughout the preserve. Cultivated fields and pastures surround Kurtz Woods, a property owned by the local Kurtz family since the 1800s. Brothers Earl and Clarence Kurtz donated the land to the Conservancy in 1980. Neighbors to the preserve assist Conservancy staff with land management activities.

Even before acquisition by the Conservancy, the preserve served as an outdoor laboratory for plant ecologists, naturalists and other University of Wisconsin scientists. It continues to be used as such and as a site for field trips by various groups.

Protected: 31 acres. Southeastern Wisconsin. Located in Ozaukee County just south of Saukville in the Town of Grafton. Designated a State Natural Area. Owned and managed by The Nature Conservancy of Wisconsin.

Directions: From intersection of State Hwy 33 and Cty Hwy O in Saukville, travel south on Cty O approximately 1 mile to intersection with Cedar Sauk Road; turn west onto Cedar Sauk Road. Travel about 0.5 mile to first access road on south past railroad crossing (use dirt road, not gravel driveway). Travel south about 0.25 mile on access road (along field edge) and park along access road. Walk south along access road, then west along edge of field to northeast corner of preserve.

Visitor Access: Open year-round. No trails. Easy hiking through woods; some rolling hills.

Lulu Lake Preserve

Mukwonago River, Lulu Lake Preserve

Lulu Lake glitters amidst the rich marshes of the upper Mukwonago River watershed in the Kettle Moraine region of southeastern Wisconsin. In terms of species richness and water quality, this 86-acre kettle lake, including its watershed, is one of the highest quality natural areas in the state.

The Conservancy's Lulu Lake Preserve, located on the west side of the lake and encompassing 631 acres, provides habitat for diverse and rare natural elements. These include open stands of oak trees, intact wetland communities, and several rare and endangered plant and animal species.

Fourteen different types of natural communities are protected at Lulu Lake Preserve. Among the rarest are the oak openings, which occur on the preserve's sprawling uplands. Distinguished by widely spaced, spreading-branched oaks with an understory of prairie grasses and wildflowers, oak openings are now a rarity. Before agricultural settlement there were more than 5.5 million acres of oak openings in Wisconsin;

now only about 500 acres survive. Between 50 and 80 of these acres are found around Lulu Lake. The Conservancy is using fire and manual removal of non-native plants to restore and maintain the oak openings at the preserve.

The wetlands at Lulu Lake are diverse and of high quality. Kettle depression bogs, sedge meadows, and calcareous fens occur on the preserve. Calcareous fens are rare plant communities bathed by calcium-rich ground water. Water from springs carries calcium and magnesium from dolomite bedrock to the marsh. Plants that tolerate these chemicals thrive at Lulu Lake. Some of these are uncommon in Wisconsin and rare in the Midwest; they include the lesser fringed gentian, Ohio goldenrod, and grass-of-Parnassus.

The slow-moving waters of the Mukwonago River are home to several rare fish species, including the longear sunfish. In the lake are glacial relict fish that require clear, deep lake water, such as the blackchin shiner and the Iowa darter. Of the 150 fish species native to Wisconsin, 59 can be found in Lulu Lake and the Mukwonago River.

The most endangered plant species in the Lulu Lake uplands is the northern kittentail, found in numerous locations at the site. This intriguing plant has a rosette of ground-hugging hairy leaves and in the spring produces foot high flowering stems that resemble kittens' tails.

Help Wanted: Exotic Plant Removal

Exotic plant species, those which are not native to a particular region, have invaded many of Wisconsin's prairies, forests, and wetlands. Some of these plants were brought in intentionally as ornamentals for landscaping, while the seeds of others were brought in accidentally on livestock and equipment, and in wool. Exotic species often thrive when introduced into a new community because their natural enemies were left behind in their native land. Unchecked, an exotic species can outcompete native species and dominate an area. The Nature Conservancy uses a number of means to control these invasive plants at its preserves including burning, pulling by hand, and careful herbicide application.

Garlic mustard, a biennial herb, is a good example of such a plant. Originally brought from Europe for its supposed medicinal properties, garlic mustard can invade forests and shade out native wildflowers. Because garlic mustard and other exotic plants are difficult to control once they get established, TNC staff and volunteers work hard to eradicate them as soon as they turn up and to keep them from spreading to new areas. If you'd like to help in the fight against exotic species, give our Volunteer Coordinator a call at (608) 251-8140.

Lulu Lake Preserve continued

Other significant wildlife species are Cooper's hawks, migrating ospreys, and nesting pairs of sandhill cranes. Many other species of birds, as well as frogs, mussels, plants, and insects also occur at the preserve.

The rare species cited above may be only a small sample of those that actually survive at Lulu Lake, since the area has yet to be thoroughly inventoried. For example, Blanchard's cricket frog was once common and may still be present. The mollusk community holds great promise of harboring rare clams. Several plant and animal inventories are currently underway at the site.

In addition to being a significant site ecologically, the Lulu Lake Preserve is an important area for scientific research. It has been used as an outdoor laboratory by researchers interested in oak openings, the hydrology of sedge meadows and fens, and rare species of fish, amphibians, reptiles, and butterflies.

Protection of Lulu Lake has been accomplished by The Nature Conservancy, the Wisconsin Department of Natural Resources State Natural Areas Program, private landowners, and private industry working together. The Conservancy made its first acquisition at Lulu Lake in 1986 and currently owns 631 acres.

Protected: 1,048 acres. Southeastern Wisconsin. Located in Walworth and Waukesha counties. Dedicated as a State Natural Area. Owned and managed by The Nature Conservancy of Wisconsin (631 acres). Adjacent protected lands (417 acres) are owned and managed by the Wisconsin Department of Natural Resources and private landowners.

Visitor Access: Special Access Only. Contact the Conservancy office for more information.

Sora

Mink River Estuary

Mink River

Mink River Estuary is a rare natural sanctuary—one of the few high quality estuaries remaining in this country. It is a wetland ecosystem that supports dozens of wildlife and plant species. An estuary is an area created when river water mixes with water from large lakes or the ocean. As a spawning habitat and source of organic detritus, these productive estuaries are vital to the Lake Michigan ecosystem. But they are fragile. Most estuaries along the Great Lakes have been destroyed because they cannot easily share precious shoreline with human development.

The Mink River Estuary is considered one of the most "pristine" of its kind. It begins at the alkaline spring-fed headwaters of the Mink River and empties into nearby Rowley's Bay. It is an important spawning ground for fish and a critical migration site for birds. More than 200 bird species may pass through the area annually. Blue-winged teal, mallards, wood ducks, and black ducks are present as nesting pairs, along with great blue herons, black terns, black-crowned night-herons, herring gulls, American bitterns, northern harriers, and common loons. In late summer and fall, double-crested cormorants and red-breasted mergansers can be seen, and there is evidence of habitation by the bald eagle and sandhill crane.

Wetlands' wildlife found at Mink River include beaver, porcupine, muskrat, raccoon, and white-tailed deer. A variety of native snakes and frogs also inhabit the area.

The diverse vegetation in the estuary features communities from white cedar swamps to wild rice marshes. Two state-threatened species are found here: the dune thistle and the dwarf lake iris. Lowland forest, dominated by white cedar, surrounds the edges of the emergent marsh.

The marsh itself is inhabited by willow, red-osier dogwood, and alder. Sedges, blue joint grass, and other emergent wetland species form the ground cover and continue through the wet meadow section. Sedge meadow and reed grass stands occur in the upstream shallow marsh portion of the wetland. Bulrush is the most ubiquitous species in the deep marsh area of the estuary. This and other deep marsh varieties serve to protect the inland communities by withstanding wave and seiche action from the lake. Many springs and intermittent streams saturate the forest floor as they feed into the river. Water lilies and water milfoil represent the submergent community of Mink River.

A history of the area reflects both Native American settlement and America's pioneer movement. Logging and farming cut a swath in the land over many generations, followed by a burgeoning tourism industry that is the Door Peninsula's chief industry today. Yet one of the most dramatic influences on the quality of the estuary is the change in lake level. As the marsh goes from exposed sediment to deep water and

Canoe and Kayak With Care in Spring

The wetlands at places like Mink River Estuary and Kangaroo Lake in Door County provide important nesting habitat for waterfowl and other bird species. Many of these birds sit on their nests from May to July. If canoeists or kayakers travel into or very close to the tall grasses, they risk flushing out the parent birds. This alerts predators to the location of the nests, greatly diminishing the survival chances of the eggs. For this reason, we ask that visitors please avoid canoeing or kayaking into or near tall grasses during these months.

Mink River Estuary continued

back again, the mix of vegetation keeps any one natural community from being preeminent.

Despite development and use, changing fortunes and careful local conservation over time helped protect the freshwater estuary in much the same condition as when it was inhabited by the Potawatomi Indians more than a century ago.

Protected: 1,465 acres. Northeastern Wisconsin. Located in Door County on the eastern shore of the peninsula at Rowley's Bay, southeast of the Village of Ellison Bay. Dedicated as a State Natural Area. Owned and managed by The Nature Conservancy of Wisconsin.

Directions: Canoe Access: From intersection of State Hwy 57 and State Hwy 42 in Sister Bay, travel 2 miles north on 42 to Cty Hwy Z; travel east on Cty Z to the Wagon Trail Campground on Rowley's Bay. Boat landing and canoe rental are available. Follow shoreline north to the mouth of the Mink River. Hiking Access: From the intersection of Hwy 57 and Hwy 42 in Sister Bay, follow Cty Hwy ZZ east 3 miles then north 2.25 miles to Cty Hwy Z. Take Cty Z east 0.5 mile to Mink River Road. Go north on Mink River Road about 1.5 miles to preserve parking area on east side of road. Access to the preserve is also available from Newport Drive (Cty Hwy NP) on the east side of the river. From Ellison Bay, travel east on Hwy 42 about 2.25 miles to Newport Drive. Take Newport Drive south 1 mile to Conservancy parking area on west side of road.

Visitor Access: Open year-round. Wetlands best viewed from canoe. Trail off of Newport Drive (Cty Hwy NP) is unmarked but well-defined. Trails off Mink River Road are unmarked and can be confusing to follow. Watch for snowmobiles on main trail in winter.

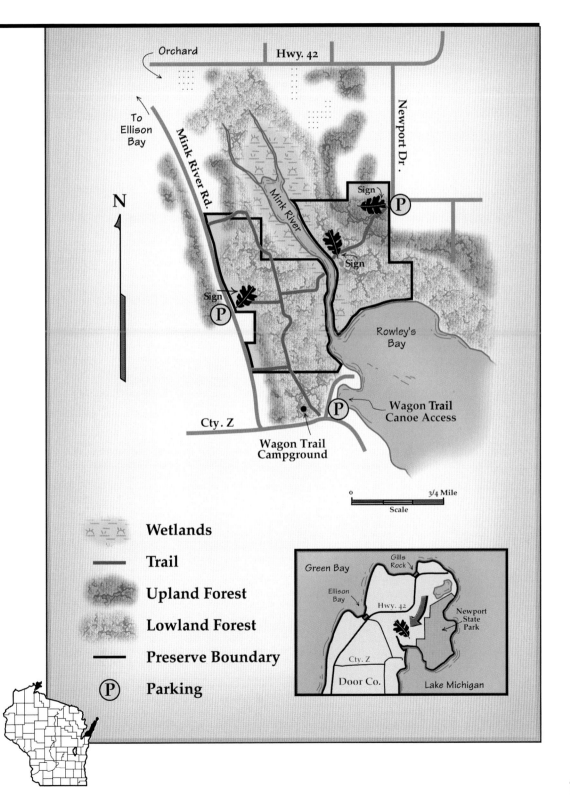

Orchard

Hwy. 42

To Ellison Bay

Mink River Rd.

Mink River

Newport Dr.

N

Sign

P

Sign

Sign

P

Rowley's Bay

Cty. Z

Wagon Trail Campground

P

Wagon Trail Canoe Access

0   3/4 Mile
Scale

Wetlands

Trail

Upland Forest

Lowland Forest

Preserve Boundary

P   Parking

Green Bay

Gills Rock

Ellison Bay

Hwy. 42

Newport State Park

Cty. Z

Door Co.

Lake Michigan

Page Creek Marsh

Sandhill cranes

Located in the central sands area of Wisconsin, Page Creek Marsh is a large wetland preserve that supports a rich diversity of plants, waterfowl, and rare meadow birds. A clear, slow-moving stream, Page Creek winds through gently rolling farmland enhanced by remnants of native prairie and oak savanna. Broad sedge meadows, marshes, and areas of open water afford habitat to a variety of rare species.

Page Creek Marsh is of particular value as a staging area for sandhill cranes during their fall migration. Luxuriant with emergent aquatic plants, the secure, deep-water habitat of the Page Creek Marsh area provides cover for large numbers of birds every season, including wood ducks, willow flycatchers, and green-backed herons. Mammals present at the preserve include beaver, red fox, coyote, and woodchuck.

The dominant plant communities at Page Creek Marsh are sandy oak savanna and sedge meadow. Prairie fens, tamarack swamps, and bogs are other community types present at Page Creek. Rare plants such as the downy willow-herb and bog reed grass thrive in the wetlands surrounding one of the lakes at the preserve. A variety of sedges and wild rice are also present at Page Creek.

Spruce bog

Page Creek Marsh continued

Green frog

In 1986, Barbara Sheehan made a gift to The Nature Conservancy of the first 71 acres at the preserve. The Conservancy has since acquired 495 acres at Page Creek Marsh, bringing the total protected acreage to 566 acres. Eventually, The Nature Conservancy hopes to safeguard more than 1,000 acres at Page Creek Marsh.

Protected: 566 acres. South-central Wisconsin. Located in Marquette County south of Packwaukee Township. Dedicated as a State Natural Area. Owned and managed by The Nature Conservancy of Wisconsin.

Directions: From Portage, drive north about 15 miles on US Hwy 51 past Endeavor to Cty Hwy D. Take Cty D east to Packwaukee; cross Buffalo Lake on Cty D and travel about 1.75 miles to Cty Hwy K. Take Cty K north about 0.5 mile to the Page Creek Marsh parking area on east side of road.

Visitor Access: Open year-round. Intermittent, unmarked, primitive trails and old roads. Narrow boardwalk over creek and through bog. Informational kiosk at entrance to preserve.

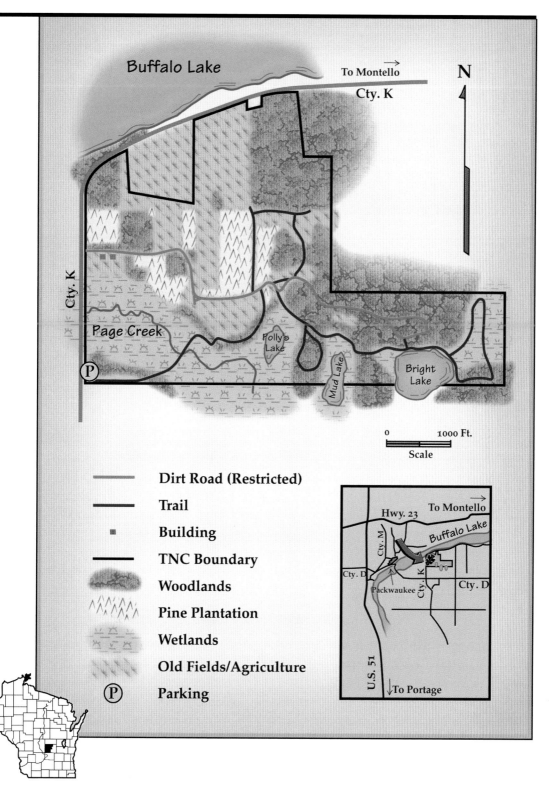

Buffalo Lake

To Montello →

Cty. K

N

Cty. K

Page Creek

Polly's Lake

Mud Lake

Bright Lake

0   1000 Ft.

Scale

—————— **Dir Road (Restricted)**

—————— **Trail**

▪ **Building**

—————— **TNC Boundary**

  Woodlands

∧∧∧∧ **Pine Plantation**

  Wetlands

  Old Fields/Agriculture

ⓟ **Parking**

Hwy. 23

To Montello →

Cty. M

Buffalo Lake

Cty. D

Packwaukee

Cty. K

Cty. D

U.S. 51

↓To Portage

Pickerel Lake Fen

Pickerel Lake Fen

There is something special about Pickerel Lake Fen. This unspoiled community is among the rarest wetland types found in North America and one of the few under conservation protection. Several rare or endangered species are protected here, some in such abundance as to belie their endangered status. Because of its rich natural history, Pickerel Lake Fen is dedicated as a State Natural Area.

The preserve is characterized by a high-quality calcareous fen sloping from a glacial ridge and an oak opening along the western boundary. A sizable population of rare beaked spike-rush dominates the fen. Dozens of northern kittentails, a state-endangered species, are present along with pitcher plants, seldom seen in "salt marsh" environments like this. Ciliated brome grass, Canada bluejoint grass, willows, and other wetland species thrive in the surrounding marshland. A diverse emergent aquatic community is evident along the uneven shoreline of the 27-acre spring-fed Pickerel Lake that lies to the north just beyond the present preserve boundary.

The wildlife of Pickerel Lake Fen add to the unique nature of this preserve. The rare Blanding's turtle lives here and sandhill cranes are known to nest among the

Fen Facts

Fens are a rare wetland type found primarily in the southern half of Wisconsin. Fens, and the plant community they support, are dependent on a geographical feature not found in great abundance—natural springs. As a result, fens have never been very common. Because the spring waters pass through limestone on their way to the surface, fens have high levels of calcium and are often called calcareous fens. This calcium-laden water results in a unique soil chemistry that supports a very specialized plant community. Among the plants found in fens are grass-of-Parnassus, lesser fringed gentian, bog arrow grass, and Ohio goldenrod.

Fens are susceptible to destruction by disruption of their water source. As a result, the fen community has been reduced to 20 percent of its original acreage in Wisconsin and is considered rare in the state.

cattails along the lake's edge. In the lake itself, starhead topminnows, an uncommon fish on the state's endangered species list, are seen in large numbers.

The pristine quality of Pickerel Lake Fen exists because the area is left largely undisturbed. Grazing and cutting on the adjacent lands have long since ceased, allowing valuable prairie habitat to reestablish along the northern oak-tree border. The Conservancy has owned and managed the land since it was donated in 1985 by Gerald and Signe Emmerich and Roy and Eleanor Muth. They made their gifts after first voluntarily registering their tracts with The Nature Conservancy. The preserve includes a conservation easement donated by the Emmerichs to serve as a protection for the calcareous fen community.

Protected: 46.5 acres. Southeastern Wisconsin. Located in Walworth County. Dedicated as a State Natural Area. Owned and managed by The Nature Conservancy of Wisconsin.

Visitor Access: Special Access only. Contact the Conservancy office for more information.

Quincy Bluff & Wetlands

Located in the Central Sands Natural Division of Wisconsin, Quincy Bluff & Wetlands Preserve is a remnant of the Wisconsin wilderness before European settlement.

Quincy Bluff, a 2-mile-long sandstone outcrop, rises 200 feet above the lake bed of the now extinct Glacial Lake Wisconsin. The bluff is dominated by northern dry forest of red and white oaks and white and red pines, with a predominantly Pennsylvania sedge understory. Prairie species, such as lead plant and butterfly weed, are found in open areas on the bluff.

The lower ridges of Quincy Bluff support pine-oak barrens—sandy areas dominated by open stretches of grass and low shrubs and sparsely timbered with pine and "scrub" oak. Once maintained by natural fires and burning by Native Americans, barrens are an increasingly rare natural community in Wisconsin. The Conservancy is restoring the pine-oak barrens at Quincy Bluff & Wetlands Preserve by reintroducing fire to the landscape.

The pine-oak barrens provide habitat for a rare tiger beetle and for larger animals like the bobcat. Quincy Bluff also has excellent potential as habitat for the federally-endangered Karner blue butterfly, whose larvae may feed on the wild lupine at the preserve.

A mesa of Cambrian sandstone known as Lone Rock lies to the northeast of Quincy Bluff. Sheer exposures of bedrock support cliff flora including bristly sarsaparilla and harebell. Rocky outcrops are likely turkey vulture roosting sites. From the top of Lone Rock, one can see for miles in all directions.

Occupying the glacial plain is a complex mosaic of conifer swamp, northern and southern sedge meadows, and shrub-carr (shrubby wetland), punctuated by sandy ridges of pine and oak. The wetlands provide excellent habitat for sandhill cranes and northern harriers. Several rare plant species dwell here, including meadow beauty, cross milkwort, and the state-endangered netted nut-rush.

In 1990, The Nature Conservancy began its involvement at Quincy Bluff with the purchase of 1,564 acres of the glacial lake bed and part of Quincy Bluff from local landowners and farmers. In November of 1992, The Nature Conservancy acquired an additional 1,663 acres at Quincy Bluff, the largest land acquisition in the Wisconsin Chapter's history, in a three-way trade with a paper company and a local private landowner. This acquisition made it possible for the Conservancy to manage Quincy Bluff & Wetlands Preserve on a landscape scale.

View of the wetlands from Quincy Bluff

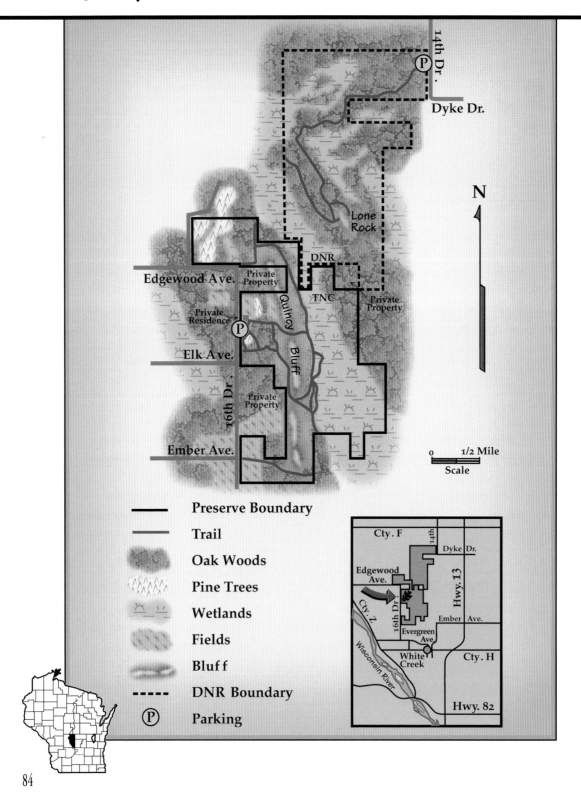

N

Lone Rock

14th Dr.

Dyke Dr.

DNR

Edgewood Ave.

Private Property

TNC

Private Property

Private Residence

Quincy Bluff

Elk Ave.

16th Dr.

Private Property

Ember Ave.

0   1/2 Mile
Scale

	Preserve Boundary
	Trail
	Oak Woods
	Pine Trees
	Wetlands
	Fields
	Bluff
	DNR Boundary
P	Parking

Cty. F
14th
Dyke Dr.
Edgewood Ave.
Hwy. 13
16th Dr.
Cty. Z
Ember Ave.
Evergreen Ave.
White Creek
Cty. H
Wisconsin River
Hwy. 82

Bobcat

In April 1993, the Conservancy transferred 1,633 acres to the Wisconsin Department of Natural Resources to establish the Quincy Bluff & Wetlands State Natural Area. The Nature Conservancy continues to own and manage 1,665 acres at the preserve.

Protected: 1,665 acres (TNC) and 3,000 acres (DNR). South-central Wisconsin. Located in Adams County south of Adams and Friendship. Dedicated as a State Natural Area. Owned and managed by The Nature Conservancy of Wisconsin and the Wisconsin Department of Natural Resources.

Directions: From Wisconsin Dells, travel north 14.4 miles on State Hwy 13 to Cty Hwy H. Turn west and proceed 2.4 miles through White Creek. Turn north onto 16th Avenue, then west onto Evergreen Avenue and north onto 16th Drive. Continue 2.2 miles to the Quincy Bluff parking area on the east side of the road.

Visitor Access: Unmarked logging roads and firebreaks loop around the bluff and may be used for hiking. Informational kiosk in the parking area.

Schluckebier Sand Prairie

Schluckebier Sand Prairie in summer

When white settlers first came to Wisconsin's Sauk Prairie area in the 1840s, prairie covered some 13,000 acres of the landscape that spread before them. Those early vistas of tall grass and colorful wildflowers stretching beyond the horizon are smaller now and merge into a scene of woods and farmland. Schluckebier Sand Prairie is an important remnant of dry prairie containing more than 158 species of prairie plants. Over half a century ago, it too was under the plow. But the sandy soil did not respond well to cultivation and it was soon left to self-restoration. The land became prairie once again.

Schluckebier Sand Prairie lies close to the glacial boundary of the driftless, or unglaciated, area of Wisconsin. The fact that it is a naturally restored community makes this preserve of special interest to the Conservancy. The rare prairie bush clover grows here, a prairie plant not seen in Wisconsin for some ninety years until 1969, when it was discovered in three localities, including Schluckebier.

The eight-acre northern section of the preserve is a significant tallgrass prairie that effectively recreates—though on a small scale—the majesty of this prairie community. Statuesque species such as big bluestem and Indian grass dominate the landscape of prairie vegetation. A variety of sedges and asters are found in both sites along with blazing star, evening primrose, catchfly, goat's beard, red sorrel, and other native plants.

Careful management over the years has lessened the encroachment of trees such as black locust, cherry, and aspen along the preserve boundaries. Nonetheless, the bordering woods encourage a healthy bird population here. Mourning dove, indigo bunting, dickcissel, bobolink, and cedar waxwing have been sighted.

The Conservancy acquired the Schluckebier preserve in two transactions, as a gift and through a trade. In 1969, area native Donald Kindschi purchased a 20-acre parcel in the southern site from the Schluckebier family, who had owned it for a hundred years. He then donated the land to the Conservancy. In 1976, a neighboring farmer traded the northern sand barrens tract and an easement through the locust woods for a 7-acre section of still-farmable land in the southeast corner of the original section.

Schluckebier Sand Prairie—two tracts separated by a road and 200 yards of farm and forest—represents the most secure prairie remnant within miles. Careful management encourages the spread of native prairie species on the property. The diversity and history of this preserve have already made it an important source of seed for prairie community restoration at other area sites.

Protected: 23 acres. Southwestern Wisconsin. Located in Sauk County west of Prairie du Sac. The preserve is divided into two tracts of natural prairie which are situated on either side of a county road. Owned and managed by The Nature Conservancy of Wisconsin.

Directions: From the intersection of US Hwy 12 and Cty Hwy PF near Prairie du Sac, travel west on Cty PF for 1.5 miles to a farm lane. Turn south onto farm lane and park along side of lane. The preserve is in two sections. One section (over 14 acres) lies south of the road and another section (over 8 acres) is located north of the road. The farm lane marks the eastern edge of the south section. To reach the north section, walk west about 0.25 mile through the prairie to a field edge, cross Cty PF and walk approximately 200 yards through a black locust woods to the prairie.

Visitor Access: Open year-round. No trails.

Shivering Sands

Arbter Lake at Shivering Sands

The Shivering Sands wetland complex may be the largest, contiguous cedar swamp in Wisconsin. Located on Lake Michigan just north of Sturgeon Bay, the area is exceptional in both size and natural community diversity.

The 3,400-acre complex encompasses three lakes, several streams and springs, forested sand dunes, lowland conifer forest, sedge meadows, and fens. The variety of natural communities provides excellent habitat for several rare plants and myriad wildlife.

Dunes, Schwartz, and Arbter lakes are shallow and fringed with cattails, rushes, and sedges, and scattered tamaracks and white cedars. Many of the plants in these wetlands, such as shrubby cinquefoil and twig rush, are typical of alkaline fens. The largest of the lakes at 81 acres, Dunes Lake receives the majority of its water from Donlan's Creek, a slow, deep-flowing creek to the north. This shallow lake is drained to the south by the narrower, more swift-flowing Shivering Sands Creek. Springs, which discharge from the dolomite bedrock that underlies the Shivering Sands area, feed several of the streams and Dunes Lake.

The large central white cedar swamp surrounding the three undeveloped lakes is rich in rare plants. Orchids flower amidst the mosses and downed trees. The fen-like communities found on the lake edges harbor such rare plants as tussock bulrush and coast sedge. Dwarf lake iris, a state- and federally-threatened species, blooms in the upland conifer forest adjacent to the cedar swamp.

Forests of beech, red maple, hemlock, and white pine are found on higher ground at Shivering Sands. Yellow birch, balsam fir, and white spruce are common on the remnant beach ridges near Glidden Drive at the eastern edge of the complex.

The diversity of communities at Shivering Sands supports an impressive suite of mammals, including short-tailed and masked shrews, fisher, otter, red fox, black bear, snowshoe hare, mink, and possibly bobcat. More than 110 different bird species also use the site. Black terns as well as sandhill cranes are regular breeders on Dunes Lake, and the forest is home to woodpeckers, warblers, and thrushes. Spring peepers, wood frogs, and blue-spotted salamanders are just a few of the amphibians that thrive at Shivering Sands.

The Nature Conservancy began its work in the Shivering Sands area in 1984 with the first bird and plant inventories. In July 1991, the Conservancy entered into an agreement with a landowner at Shivering Sands to manage 190 acres. Since that time, the Conservancy has acquired four parcels of land at the site totaling 192 acres. These parcels contain part of the lowland cedar swamp, a fen, forested sand ridges, and inter-dunal wetlands. The Conservancy will continue to work with local landowners, land trusts, and property owners associations to protect this nationally significant wetland area.

Protected: 192 acres. Northeastern Wisconsin. Located on Lake Michigan northeast of Sturgeon Bay in Door County. Owned and managed by The Nature Conservancy of Wisconsin.

Visitor Access: Special Access only. Contact the Conservancy office for more information.

Snapper Memorial Prairie

Snapper Memorial Prairie is a remnant of what was once a 2,500-acre low prairie in the Crawfish River floodplain. Twenty acres of the prairie were never plowed as was the land around them. Instead, the owners mowed these acres for hay and burned them in the fall—treatment that helped preserve many prairie plant species.

A rich collection of low prairie plants represents the more common species that populate Snapper Prairie. Big bluestem, little bluestem, prairie dock, and prairie dropseed also grow here. Many showy prairie forbs, like the blazing star, coneflower, and compass plant, add color to the site. At least two threatened plants—prairie Indian plantain and prairie milkweed—are found at the prairie. The clay soil of the lowland prairie means moisture conditions can dramatically change the look of this preserve from dry to flooded, depending on rainfall.

Snapper Memorial Prairie is also home to many native birds and mammals. Upland sandpipers and bobolinks have nested on the prairie—an unusual situation due to the small size and isolation of this prairie remnant. Savanna sparrows and eastern meadowlarks are a fairly common sight here. Small mammals, including meadow voles, shrews, and white-footed mice, are abundant at this protected area between fields of soybeans and corn.

Since the area was settled in the 1870s, up to the time of sale to the Conservancy in 1979, the land that is Snapper Memorial Prairie had been owned by one family, the Millers. Funds for the purchase were donated by the children of a Milwaukee couple as a memorial to their parents, Arthur and Albena Snapper.

Protected: 28 acres. Southeastern Wisconsin. Located in Jefferson County north of Lake Mills. Dedicated as a State Natural Area. Owned and managed by The Nature Conservancy of Wisconsin.

Directions: From Lake Mills, follow State Hwy 89 north 2.5 miles, then Cty Hwy G north 3.2 miles to a field access lane on east side of road. Lane is marked with fire number N8696. Follow the lane 0.5 mile to the prairie. Park in small fenced-in parking area at southwest corner of the preserve.

Visitor Access: Open from May to October (access lane is not plowed in the winter months). No trails. Poison ivy is abundant in northernmost 8 acres of the preserve. This is a wet prairie and is frequently inundated with water. Access road is flooded after heavy rainfall.

Prairie milkweed

Spring Green Preserve

Spring Green Preserve

I t is known as the "Wisconsin Desert," this place where forest meets bluff and bluff levels off into plains and dunes. Spring Green Preserve is one of the region's finest examples of dry sand prairie grading into dry lime prairie on steep dolomite cliffs where mixing occurs with southern mesic forest. Situated on an ancient terrace of the Wisconsin River that merges into the limey bluffs to the immediate north, the preserve is located in the driftless, or unglaciated, area of the state. Spring Green Preserve recalls the desert land of the American West, a land of cacti and lizards, sand dunes and dry grasses.

This preserve harbors some of Wisconsin's rarest plant communities, including sand prairie, dry bluff prairie, and black oak barrens. All of these communities, which once covered thousands of acres in the state, are now almost completely gone. They provide habitat for many rare and unusual plants and animals.

One of these species is prickly pear cactus, which is not common in the state but is abundant at Spring Green Preserve. The large, fleshy pads and stems of the cactus store water and the plant's waxy coating retains moisture, both important adaptations for this dry environment. The cactus blooms in late June, producing many large, pale yellow flowers. Other plants common to Spring Green's prairies include little bluestem, dwarf dandelion, lead plant, and compass plant.

Spring Green Preserve is home to a diversity of wildlife, including reptiles, small mammals and birds. One of the interesting mammals found at the preserve is the eastern pocket gopher. This solitary creature digs and forms tunnels about one foot below the surface of the soil. These tunnels provide shelter for the gopher as well as other animals at the preserve. The gopher's digging also enriches the soil by mixing it with plant material and oxygen. Spring Green Preserve also provides habitat for grassland birds,

Volunteer Emily Earley assisting with a prescribed burn

Fire as a Conservation Tool

In Wisconsin, The Nature Conservancy has been using fire as a management tool on preserve land since the early 1970s. Controlled fires to promote appropriate habitat—known as "prescribed burns"—are an important aspect of our land management program.

Fully half of our 55 Wisconsin preserves harbor fire-derived and dependent plant communities such as prairie, savanna, oak woodland, and sedge meadow. Conservancy staff and volunteers burn these sites on a rotating schedule designed to mimic natural fires and to maintain conditions that will promote the birds, insects, plants, and countless other life forms that depend on a specific habitat type. Fire returns nutrients to the soil, allows the sun to reach and warm the soil and thus stimulate plant growth, allows dormant seeds to germinate, provides important habitat niches for many plants and animals, and reduces competition by exotic (non-native) species. When trained TNC staff and volunteers conduct a burn at a preserve, they are playing an important role in maintaining a natural community.

which are declining in number due to habitat fragmentation and loss on both their breeding and wintering grounds. Some of the grassland birds found at the preserve include the eastern and western meadowlarks, vesper and lark sparrows, and the dickcissel.

Among the most unusual animals at Spring Green Preserve are the invertebrates. Some are insects found nowhere else in Wisconsin: a cicada with a lisping call (*Diceroprocta vitripennis*), one of five cicadas at Spring Green Preserve; the subtropical *Megacephala virginica*, one of seven tiger beetles recorded; and several rare leafhoppers. Ten species of wolf spiders occur at the preserve. Wolf spiders hunt at night, either by waiting near their burrows until insects pass near or by moving actively about.

The Spring Green Preserve began as part of a 480-acre joint management agreement between The Nature Conservancy, the Head Foundation, the Wisconsin Natural Areas Preservation Council, and local landowners. The Conservancy acquired its first tract of land at Spring Green Preserve in 1971. Today the Conservancy owns 429 acres at the preserve and manages an additional 161 acres in cooperation with an adjacent landowner.

The Conservancy works with the State Natural Areas Program, local landowners, and scientists from the University of Wisconsin to protect this unique community of plants and animals. The Conservancy and its partners are working to maintain and restore the sand prairie/oak barrens ecosystem of the Spring Green Preserve, which is frequently used for education and research. Land management activities at the preserve include the removal of red cedars, which invade the prairies and shade out native plant species, and the use of prescribed burns to suppress competing trees and shrubs and stimulate growth of native grasses and wildflowers.

Protected: 590 acres. Southwestern Wisconsin. Located in Sauk County just north of Spring Green in the Wisconsin River valley. A 260-acre section of the Spring Green Preserve is designated a State Natural Area. Owned and managed by The Nature Conservancy of Wisconsin.

Directions: From the intersection of US Hwy 14 and State Hwy 23 near Spring Green, travel north on 23 for 0.5 mile to intersection with Jones Road; travel east on Jones Road for 0.75 mile to preserve. Turn onto a dirt access road marked Angelo Lane, just past driveway with fire number E5196A.

Visitor Access: Open year-round. Informational kiosk in parking area. Self-guided trail. Do not hike on the bluff.

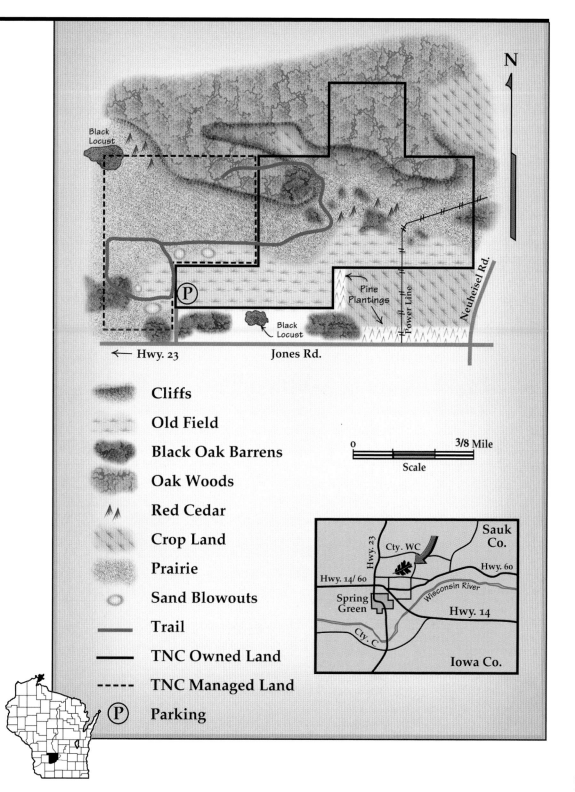

N

Black
Locust

Pine
Plantings

Power Line

Neuheisel Rd.

Black
Locust

← Hwy. 23

Jones Rd.

Cliffs

Old Field

Black Oak Barrens

Oak Woods

Red Cedar

Crop Land

Prairie

Sand Blowouts

Trail

TNC Owned Land

TNC Managed Land

(P) Parking

0   3/8 Mile
Scale

Sauk
Co.

Hwy. 23

Cty. WC

Hwy. 60

Hwy. 14/ 60

Wisconsin River

Spring
Green

Hwy. 14

Cty. C

Iowa Co.

Thomson Memorial Prairie

Monarch butterfly

Located on the border between Dane and Iowa counties in Wisconsin's Driftless Area, Thomson Memorial Prairie is a remnant of the past. Many hilltops and steep slopes of southwestern Wisconsin were covered with dry prairie vegetation prior to settlement. Today only a few remain, and Thomson Memorial Prairie is one of them.

This dry prairie, surrounded on all sides by farmland, probably only survives because the limestone bedrock beneath the soil lies too close to the surface to permit cultivation.

A diverse natural community thrives at Thomson Memorial Prairie; more than 68 species of plants grow there and 34 species of birds nest or feed there. Rare plants, such as pomme de prairie and green milkweed, thrive among a profusion of other prairie grasses and wildflowers. Big bluestem, porcupine grass, yellow-star grass, pasque flower, and bird-foot violet are just a few of the many prairie plants that grace the undulating landscape at Thomson Memorial Prairie.

Thomson Memorial Prairie also provides habitat for many grassland bird species. Red-winged blackbirds, dickcissels, and eastern meadowlarks are common. Upland

lazingstar and sunflowers

sandpipers, bobolinks, loggerhead shrikes, and Bell's vireos have also been seen there.

Many butterfly species also rely on this habitat, including monarchs, tiger swallowtails, and various species of skippers and sulphurs.

The Conservancy became involved in protecting the area, called Thousand's Rock Point Prairies, in 1964 when it received a donation of 3 acres of land from Stacy and Mildred Collins in honor of their father, Christian W. Thousand, who farmed the nearby land for many years. This was the first land donation ever made to the Wisconsin Chapter of The Nature Conservancy. In 1987, John and Olive Thomson, longtime friends and stewards of the prairie, established a memorial fund in honor of their son Douglas to assist with acquisition of another 27 acres at the site. The Conservancy named the area Thomson Memorial Prairie in recognition of their conservation efforts. Today the Conservancy owns and manages 175 acres at Thomson Memorial Prairie.

Little remains of Wisconsin's once extensive grasslands. Those that have managed to survive, like Thomson Memorial Prairie, are small, isolated, and fragmented. In order to ensure their viability into the future, these prairie remnants must be carefully managed and expanded to recreate a larger grassland ecosystem.

The Nature Conservancy continues to acquire land at Thomson Memorial Prairie. With the help of volunteers, the Conservancy is working to restore degraded prairie and agricultural land surrounding the preserve through a combination of planting, prescribed burning, and exotic species control. In this way, The Nature Conservancy continues its work to not only save a small remnant of Wisconsin's tallgrass prairie but to restore some of what has been lost.

Protected: 175 acres. Southwestern Wisconsin. Located in both Dane and Iowa counties southwest of Blue Mounds. Owned and managed by The Nature Conservancy of Wisconsin.

Directions: Travel on US Hwy 18/151 west from Mt. Horeb to the intersection with Cty Hwy F on the southwestern edge of Blue Mounds. Turn south on Cty F for about 1 mile to intersection with Cty Hwy Z. Continue on Cty F, by turning west, for a half mile. Preserve is on northwest side of road. Park in small fenced parking lot or along side of the road.

Visitor Access: Open year-round, except in winter months when plowed snow prevents off-road parking. No trails. Poison ivy is abundant.

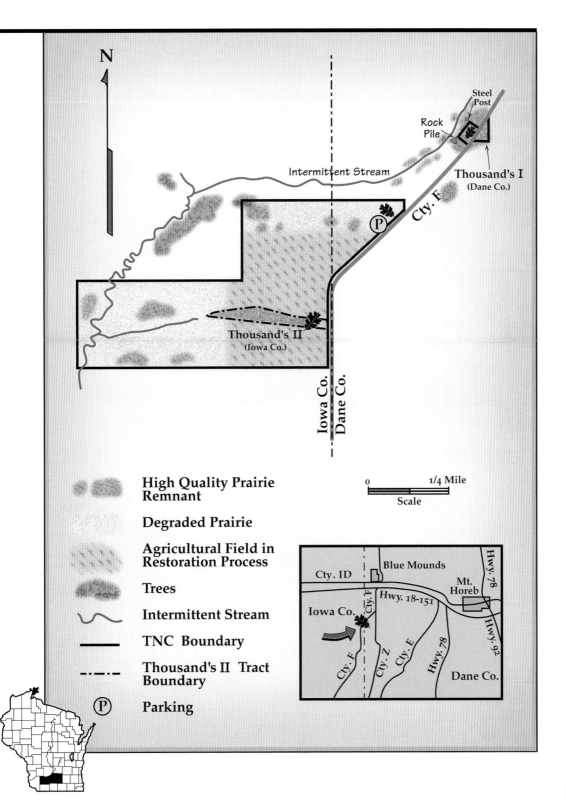

N

Steel
Post

Rock
Pile

Intermittent Stream

Thousand's I
(Dane Co.)

Cty. F

P

Thousand's II
(Iowa Co.)

Iowa Co.
Dane Co.

High Quality Prairie
Remnant

Degraded Prairie

Agricultural Field in
Restoration Process

Trees

Intermittent Stream

TNC Boundary

Thousand's II Tract
Boundary

P   Parking

0   1/4 Mile
Scale

Blue Mounds

Cty. ID

Hwy. 18-151

Mt.
Horeb

Hwy. 78

Iowa Co.

Cty. F

Cty. Z

Cty. E

Hwy. 78

Hwy. 92

Dane Co.

Cty. F

Waubesa Wetlands

Waubesa Wetlands is part of one of the most studied and valued water habitats in Wisconsin, covering more than 700 acres. Past studies have investigated the geology of the land, the diversity of the plant and animal life, the biological productivity of the site and many other aspects of what is a remarkably undisturbed wetland. The Nature Conservancy tracts, in particular, contain several state-threatened species and uncommon community types.

Long termed a "living museum" of Wisconsin's native plant and animal communities, the Waubesa Wetlands is thought by ecologists to have once been a bay of Lake Waubesa. In its present incarnation, the wetlands include springs, sedge meadows, floating mats, and a fen. The water source here is not the lake, despite its proximity, but numerous small springs that erupt near the upland edge of the wetlands to provide a continuous flow of clear, cool water. One of the most impressive is Bogholt Deep Spring, part of a 40-acre tract donated by Carl and Julia Bogholt. The spring originates 12 feet beneath Deep Spring Creek from a cave lined with filamentous algae and purple-colored sulfur bacteria.

Southern sedge meadow, a state-threatened community, is found here. The meadow features bluejoint grass and tussock sedge amid a scattering of sawgrass sedge, cattails, and bur-reed. A fen community of brome grass, aster, goldenrod, and sage willow thrives in the cold, limy spring water of the wetlands. Red-osier dogwood, pussy willow, and bog birch are part of a shrub-carr community located along the western edge of the Conservancy tract. State-threatened or uncommon plants at Waubesa include lesser fringed gentian, small water parsnip, and yellow monkey flower.

Though visitors find it difficult to traverse the marshy terrain, it provides good habitat for many species of waterfowl and other migrating birds. Waubesa is an important nesting area for the sandhill crane, great blue heron, American bittern, Canada goose, and American coot, as well as the blue-gray gnatcatcher, common yellowthroat, and common grackle. Along the creek beds, a thriving population of Blanding's turtles, another state-threatened species, is found. The waters of the Waubesa Wetlands preserve also provide a major fish spawning area, especially for northern pike in early to mid-spring.

The Conservancy has acquired land for the Waubesa Wetlands preserve in the form of gifts and purchases since 1974. The sustained high quality of this preserve is due in large part to the support of many area residents and landowners who recognize the value of preserving such an important habitat.

The Conservancy continues to work closely in a conservation partnership with the Town of Dunn, Dane County, the Wisconsin Department of Natural Resources, and the Southern Wisconsin Wetlands Association in protecting the integrity of the Waubesa Wetlands.

Common yellowthroat

Waubesa Wetlands

Waubesa Wetlands

Protected: 194 acres. Southwestern Wisconsin. Located in Dane County southeast of Madison at the southwestern end of Lake Waubesa. Dedicated as a State Natural Area. This is a joint project between The Nature Conservancy of Wisconsin and the Wisconsin Department of Natural Resources Natural Areas Program. Both organizations own and cooperatively manage land in the area. Dane County Natural Heritage Foundation also owns land in the area.

Directions: From Madison, travel south on US Hwy 14 about 0.5 mile to the intersection with Cty Hwy MM (McCoy Road). Turn east onto MM and travel 1.25 miles to Goodland Park Road. Turn east onto Goodland Park Road and travel 0.5 mile to Larsen Road. Turn south onto Larsen Road and travel 0.5 mile to Lalor Road. Turn west onto Lalor Road and travel 0.75 mile to preserve entrance on east side of road. Park in small parking area just beyond entrance. Can also park along side of road. Walk east along access lane for 0.25 mile to reach the preserve.

Visitor Access: Open year-round. No trails. Wetlands best viewed from canoe; you can put canoe in at Goodland County Park.

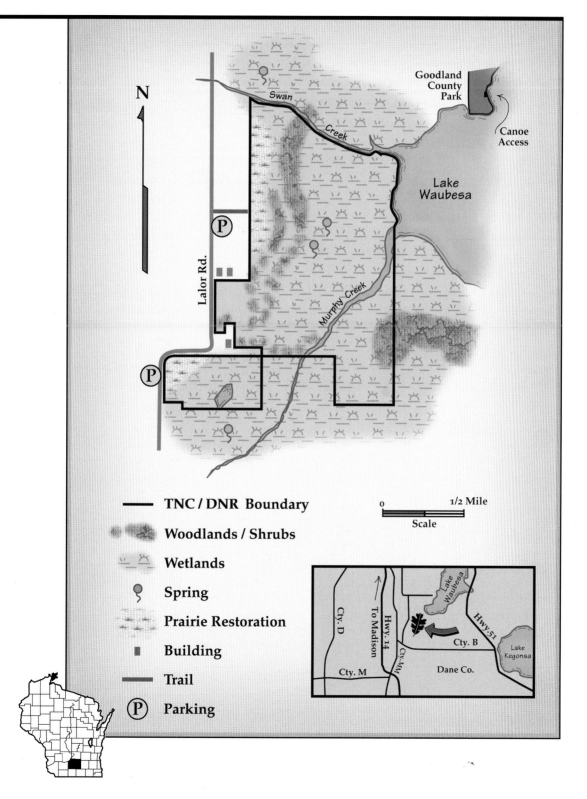

N

Swan Creek

Goodland County Park

Canoe Access

Lake Waubesa

Lalor Rd.

Murphy Creek

P

P

TNC / DNR Boundary

Woodlands / Shrubs

Wetlands

Spring

Prairie Restoration

Building

Trail

P Parking

0   1/2 Mile
Scale

Lake Waubesa

Cty. D

To Madison

Hwy. 14

Cty. MM

Cty. B

Hwy. 51

Lake Kegonsa

Cty. M

Dane Co.

Walter & Rose Zinn Preserve

Just 35 miles from downtown Milwaukee, the Walter & Rose Zinn Preserve thrives undisturbed. Acquired by the Conservancy as a gift from Rose Zinn in 1981, the site is characterized by a rare combination of two community types—pristine lake and tamarack swamp. The lakes on the preserve are encircled by some 70 acres of swamp and wet mesic forest species like white cedar, black spruce, balsam fir, and jack pine. Mosses and other swamp groundcover, such as creeping snowberry and false solomon's seal, are also found along the shoreline. Beck Lake provides safe harbor for nesting and migrating waterfowl, including wood ducks, blue-wing teal, and mallards. Walters Lake to the north supports a large fish population, including northern pike and largemouth bass.

Natural communities present at the preserve include sedge bog, southern mesic forest, swamp hardwood forest, and shrub-carr. The site harbors a fine mix of prairie grasses, dogwoods and willows, goldenrod, milkweed, sweet cicely, and wild leek. A canopy of sugar maples draws a sizable population of forest breeding birds to the Zinn Preserve, such as the cedar waxwing, wood thrush, and black-capped chickadee. The land along the lakes remains in an original undisturbed state, making it an ideal site for research by scientists at the University of Wisconsin and other research institutions.

Protected: 227 acres. Southeastern Wisconsin. Located in Washington County near Hartford in the Town of Erin. Owned and managed by The Nature Conservancy of Wisconsin.

Visitor Access: Special Access only. Contact the Conservancy office for more information.

Showy lady's-slipper

Nature Conservancy Cooperative Projects

Brule River

The Nature Conservancy of Wisconsin maintains close ties with many public agencies, private organizations, and individuals. The Conservancy often joins forces with conservation partners to secure protection of threatened natural lands. Such cooperation is necessary because financial resources for conservation would be severely limited with individual efforts alone. We could not save the natural heritage of Wisconsin without it.

Thus, we share a deep concern for the safekeeping of the biological and ecological history of Wisconsin and work together to save what we can. In some cases, the Conservancy acquires land and later transfers ownership, at cost or as a gift, to an appropriate steward such as a university or public agency. The Conservancy frequently works with the Wisconsin Department of Natural Resources and other groups to help preserve large and valuable natural areas. While the Conservancy does not own or directly manage these preserves, we include them in this guide because we're proud of the part we played in saving them.

Abraham's Woods

Abraham's Woods was the first acquisition made by The Nature Conservancy in Wisconsin. A 40-acre tract of deep woods grading into dry prairie was purchased by the Conservancy in 1961 and transferred to the University of Wisconsin-Madison soon after. Though the woods had been used as a woodlot over the past hundred years, cutting was done on a selective basis that helped preserve the overstory of trees and understory of herbs. The site was named for a previous owner, Ben Abraham, who collected maple sap here until his death.

This preserve is a remnant of a climax, or terminal, forest and dry prairie combination. It represents the landscape of pre- and early-settlement Wisconsin, a magnificent and complex woods surrounded by prairie. Large red oaks are sparse but suggest the towering trees that prevailed at one time. Sugar maple and slippery elm now dominate the forest canopy. Basswood, yellowbud hickory, hackberry, black walnut, and butternut are present in smaller numbers.

Preservation of this land has much to do with its topography. Along the western edge of the woods, a sandstone hill curves both northeastward and southeastward, leaving an amphitheater-like formation facing east. It forms a windbreak so fires that regularly consumed the surrounding prairie did not destroy the sheltered trees beyond. The dry prairie lies less than a mile south along this sandstone ridge.

Of singular value in Abraham's Woods, and one of the primary reasons for protection of this site, is the diversity of flora. Spring growth is especially rich in woodland flowers and herbs, including trillium, trout lily, spring beauty, Dutchman's-breeches, and false mermaid. Goldie's fern, an uncommon species, grows abundantly in the "amphitheater." With the passing of spring, wood nettle and jewelweed dominate the understory.

Abraham's Woods is considered one of the most stable and self-sustaining communities of its type in southern Wisconsin and, as such, is an essential teaching and research laboratory for University of Wisconsin plant and forest scientists.

Protected: 63.5 acres. Southern Wisconsin. Located in Green County 35 miles south of Madison. Owned and managed by the University of Wisconsin and used primarily for education. Contact the Director, UW-Arboretum, 1207 Seminole Hwy, Madison, WI 53713 or call (608) 262-2748 for more information on this preserve.

Archibald Lake Hemlock Forest

Ancient, towering hemlocks are the dominant feature of the 110-acre tract of land that The Nature Conservancy acquired from the descendants of the Holt Lumber Company in 1991. Hemlocks share the canopy of this old-growth forest with beech, sugar maple, yellow birch, and red and white pines. The understory is a lovely mixture of witch hazel, baneberry, beech drops, blue-bead lily, and maidenhair and wood ferns.

The property is located at the northwestern end of Archibald Lake, a 430-acre lake with numerous islands and peninsulas. The hemlock forest, lake, and surrounding wetlands provide important wildlife habitat. Rare species including the elusive pine marten, bald eagle, and red-shouldered hawk frequent the area. Other animals including red and gray fox, beaver, mink, and black bear find food and shelter there. Barred owls, common loons, pileated woodpeckers, and scarlet tanagers are just a few of the birds you may encounter on a walk through these deep woods.

The Nature Conservancy was able to purchase the land from the Holt and DeWitt families through a generous contribution from an anonymous donor. The Conservancy transferred the land to the U.S. Forest Service in April 1993. The Nicolet National Forest will continue to preserve the land in its natural state for future generations.

Adjacent to the property is a prime stand of virgin white pine known as Cathedral Pines. This land was sold to the U.S. Forest Service in the 1960s by the same family that owned the Archibald Lake Hemlock Forest. The Cathedral Pines area attracts many visitors each year to see the heron rookery perched high atop the white pines.

Protected: 110 acres. Northeastern Wisconsin. Located in Oconto County within the Nicolet National Forest. Owned and managed by the U.S. Forest Service. For more information, contact Superintendent, Nicolet National Forest, Federal Building, 68 S. Stevens Street, Rhinelander, WI 54501 or call (715) 362-1300.

Brule River

One of the Conservancy's most ambitious projects in Wisconsin depends on the cooperation of many individuals. The Brule River Conservation Easement Program is intended to bring more than 5,000 acres of one of the state's largest and highest quality forests under long-term protection. Working with local landowners, the Conservancy secured conservation easements to preserve riverbanks, swamps, and forests along the Brule as well as portions of the river itself. Under this voluntary program, private landowners agree to limit commercial development, construction, degradation of watercourses, off-road vehicle use, logging, and mining, while continuing to use their land as home sites and for compatible recreation.

Considered by some fishermen as one of the nation's top five trout fishing rivers, the Brule is pristine. This unique preserve encompasses nearly one-third of the river's length, the largest area of land within the Brule watershed that has escaped extensive and detrimental development.

The majestic upland pine forests dominate one's first impression of the Brule. The stands of old-growth red and white pines—some individual specimens perhaps more than 300 years old—are found nowhere else in the state. The tall pines provide valuable nesting habitat for the bald eagle and osprey, both of which hunt the Brule for fish.

Nine major plant communities are identified along this 9-mile stretch of northern river. A significant community at the preserve is the lowland cedar swamp community, one of the best examples of its type left in the state. Here, white bog orchids grow with a wealth of other species in a richly diverse ecosystem.

The gray wolf, an endangered species, also inhabits the Brule River area. Some 90 bird species are recorded in this nesting sanctuary, seven of them considered rare in the state: black-backed woodpecker, yellow-bellied flycatcher, Swainson's thrush, ruby-crowned kinglet, Cape May warbler, evening grosbeak, and Connecticut warbler. The diversity of life in this preserve even extends to the river's spawning beds for brook trout.

Conservancy involvement along the Brule began in 1979 with a biological analysis. Negotiations with landowners began in 1981 and continue to the present.

Protected: Protected: 4,958 acres. Northwestern Wisconsin. Located in Douglas County in the southern section of the Brule River State Forest, about 20 miles east of Superior. The Nature Conservancy of Wisconsin administers a conservation easement program to protect ecologically sensitive areas from damaging development. All acreage is privately owned. Access is by permission of landowners only or via boat on the river. Contact the Conservancy office for more information.

Cedarburg Bog

Pitcher plant

Located 8 miles west of the shore of Lake Michigan in Ozaukee County, Cedarburg Bog is one of the largest, least disturbed, and most diverse wetlands in this region of the state. It covers most of what was once a large post-glacial lake basin. When ice sheets melted in southeastern Wisconsin twelve thousand years ago, the basin was created. Gradual filling over the centuries has reduced the surface water to six small lakes. The largest, Mud Lake, is only 245 acres and quite shallow.

One of the bog's most unique features is its well-developed string, or patterned, bog. A string bog consists of a series of parallel ridges that support white cedar and tamarack, alternating with low-lying stretches of bog shrubs and sedges. It is unusual for a string bog to exist in southeastern Wisconsin. The nearest bogs of this type lie 200 miles north in Michigan, Minnesota, and Canada.

Some of the other plant communities present at Cedarburg Bog include southern swamp hardwoods, conifer swamp, sedge meadow, shrub carr, deep and shallow marsh, and floating aquatics. The large size and variety of these communities provides upland and wetland habitat for numerous birds, mammals, and unusual plants.

Mammals common to Cedarburg Bog include raccoon, muskrat, coyote, beaver, mink, white-tailed deer, river otter, and red-backed vole (a mouse that is not normally found this far south). Common nesting birds include the northern waterthrush and the white-throated sparrow. Both species are at their southernmost range limit here.

As for unusual plants, several types of "carnivorous," insect-eating plants, such as the pitcher plant, thrive in Cedarburg Bog's water-logged, low-nitrogen soils. Other plants, such as the water lily and the pickerel weed, do well in the shallow lakes.

In addition to supporting diverse and unusual plant and animal communities, the bog serves an important surface water storage and purification function. This natural value was recognized early on by respected state conservationists such as Aldo Leopold. Steps to preserve the bog were begun in 1946. In 1952, the bog was designated as one of the first State Scientific Areas and is now classified as a National Natural Landmark as well.

Close to 1,970 of the total 2,500 acres at Cedarburg Bog have been protected by a joint effort of the University of Wisconsin-Milwaukee (UWM), the Wisconsin Department of Natural Resources, and The Nature Conservancy.

Development of the UWM Field Station on the bog periphery provides outdoor laboratory facilities for many university and high school students. The bog is also open by permission to the general public for nature hikes, bird study, and research.

Protected: 395 acres. Southeastern Wisconsin. Located west of Saukville in Ozaukee County. Owned by the University of Wisconsin-Milwaukee, the Wisconsin Department of Natural Resources, and The Nature Conservancy. Contact Jim Reinartz at the UW-Milwaukee Field Station, 3095 Blue Goose Road, Saukville, WI 53080 or call (414) 675-6844 for more information.

Flambeau River

A remarkable warm-water river and forest ecosystem are preserved for all time along the upper north fork of the Flambeau River. The preserve encompasses approximately 300 feet on either side of a 12-mile stretch of the beautiful, free-flowing Flambeau. This stretch of the river is particularly valuable for its near-primitive condition as a virtually unpolluted river without a road-crossing or dam. Though the river was used for logging during the state's early history (old logging dam sites are still visible), the forest-covered riverbank and the river itself were not significantly marred by such industry. In fact, the land was purchased, in part, from industrial firms who recognized the importance of saving one of the finest natural river communities in the country.

The Flambeau River Preserve contains a fine example of Wisconsin's boreal, or far northern, forest—old-growth upland stands of white and red pine with an understory of white spruce, white cedar and balsam fir. This forest contains trees that measure as much as two- to two-and-one-half feet in diameter.

A variety of wetland communities are distributed along the river, including a large tract of wetland conifer forest dominated by white cedar and ash, elm, and red maple. Large silver maples along the river's edge are at the northern limit of their geographic range. A small spring-fed stream flows through this area, forming shallow ponds near the headwaters.

The Flambeau River Preserve provides important nesting and feeding habitat for bald eagles, ospreys, and red-shouldered hawks. The unpolluted water of the river supports rare fish species, including the river redhorse and the lake sturgeon, as well as a diverse, natural game fish community. Ruffed grouse, coyote, river otter, beaver, and black bear are among the wildlife inhabiting narrow reaches of the riverbank. An uncommon plant species at the Flambeau preserve is the small round-leaved orchis.

Land for the Flambeau River Preserve was originally purchased by the Conservancy in 1985 following more than six years of complex negotiations. It was then transferred to the Wisconsin Department of Natural Resources with deed restrictions on development. The preserve is an important area for canoeing and fishing, and its biological diversity and ecological quality make it well-suited for research and education.

Protected: 1,112 acres. Northern Wisconsin. Located in Ashland, Iron, and Rusk counties on upper north fork of river above the city of Park Falls. Owned and managed by the Wisconsin Department of Natural Resources (DNR) as a State Natural Area for research and recreation. For more information, contact the DNR at 101 S. Webster Street, Madison, WI 53707 or call (608) 266-8916.

Jackson Harbor Ridges

Facing northeast along the shoreline of Washington Island, Jackson Harbor Ridges is a small preserve that features an outstanding collection of natural communities. Beaches, lake dunes and ridges, wetlands, and forests combine to make Jackson Harbor the only beach of its kind on the islands surrounding the Door Peninsula. The beach undulates, with twelve sandy ridges separated by low wet areas known as interdunal swales. Each ridge follows the contour of an ancient shoreline of the ancestral Lake Michigan. The interdunal swale is a globally endangered natural community, and the undisturbed Great Lakes beach is globally threatened.

The ridges and swales at Jackson Harbor Ridges Preserve are host to black and white spruces and tamarack along the beach on the western edge, drier dunes that are stabilized with drought-resistant species such as little bluestem and horizontal juniper, and a mixed conifer-hardwood forest with red and white pine, white cedar, balsam fir, American beech, and various other hardwoods. The transition from dunes through boreal forest is compressed into a mere 300 feet.

A variety of rare or endangered plants thrive at Jackson Harbor Ridges including dwarf lake iris, false asphodel, Ohio goldenrod, and bird's-eye primrose.

Jackson Harbor is sheltered by Carlin's Point, a stabilized sand spit that supports a scenic grove of white pine, paper birch, and white spruce. The shallows off the point are favored resting and feeding areas for shore birds and waterfowl, including ring-billed and Bonaparte's gulls and red-breasted mergansers. Waterfowl concentrate along the Door Peninsula and frequently rest in Jackson Harbor during their spring and fall migrations.

In 1973 the Town of Washington Island purchased 39 acres along the southern boundary of Jackson Harbor and set aside the land as a natural area. The Conservancy assisted the Town with a loan to purchase the tract. Jackson Harbor Ridges was named a State Scientific Area in 1973. The Nature Conservancy acquired 43 acres known as Carlin's Point in 1988. In 1992, the Conservancy transferred the land to the Town of Washington Island to become part of the Jackson Harbor Ridges Preserve. The preserve is a fine example of the committed efforts of local citizens to safeguard one of Wisconsin's significant natural areas.

Protected: 82 acres. Northeastern Wisconsin. Located on Washington Island in Door County. Owned by the Town of Washington Island and managed by the Washington Island Natural Areas Board. Contact the Town Board Chair, Village Clerk and Treasurer's Office, (414) 847-2522, for more information.

Kenosha Sand Dunes

Kenosha Sand Dunes anchor the northern terminus of the longest and largest prairie-wetland complex east of the Mississippi River. The complex extends more than 5 miles from the Carol Beach area and the Conservancy's Chiwaukee Prairie Preserve to the swell and swale lands of northeastern Illinois.

The Conservancy acquired the property in 1994 as a gift from Wisconsin Electric Power Company in honor of Clifford F. Messinger, former chairman of the Conservancy's national Board of Governors and of the Wisconsin Chapter Board of Trustees.

Five of the most endangered natural community types of the Midwest occur in this several thousand-acre expanse. Four of these natural communities are found on the Sand Dunes tract: foredunes, backdunes, wet swales, and prairie. This mosaic of communities hosts more than 240 species of plants.

Portions of the foredunes and backdunes have been colonized by trees, including black oak and cottonwood. Other flora on the dunes includes lake shore rush, little bluestem, beach wormwood, Canada wild rye, puccoon, and evening primrose. Some of the plants you might expect to see in the wet swales and prairie include big and little bluestem, Indian grass, yellow star grass, prairie dock, and golden alexander.

Bird surveys conducted at the site show it to be important habitat for many migratory species. Raptors, such as the bald eagle, red-tailed hawk, and osprey have been seen in the area. Mammals, including the Franklin's ground squirrel, also find food and shelter there. Monarch butterflies use the prairie plants at the Dunes extensively during their fall migration.

Kenosha Sand Dunes is also significant for a deeply buried Pleistocene Ice Age forest, first discovered in the 1960s. Logs and roots of such species as ash and oak that are approximately 6,300 years old were found at the site. The dunes area was used by Native Americans as a camp site and possibly as an implement workshop, indicated by artifacts found there.

The Conservancy transferred Kenosha Sand Dunes to the Wisconsin Department of Natural Resources in January 1995 to become part of the Chiwaukee Prairie State Natural Area. The DNR will be restoring portions of the prairie at the Dunes and may use controlled burning as a management tool.

Protected: 56 acres. Southeastern Wisconsin. Located in the Village of Pleasant Prairie just south of the City of Kenosha in Kenosha County. Owned and managed by the Wisconsin Department of Natural Resources (DNR) as a State Natural Area for research and recreation. Open to visitors for hiking and nature observation. For more information, contact the DNR at 101 S. Webster Street, Madison, WI 53707 or call (608) 266-8916.

Michigan Island

Michigan Island is one of 22 Apostle Islands forming an archipelago off the northern coast of Wisconsin in Lake Superior. The beach-front portion of the Michigan Island Preserve is part of a 520-square-mile National Lakeshore area along the Bayfield Peninsula. Known today for their beauty and tourist appeal, the islands and lakeshore stand as living remnants of the Ice Age, featuring valuable examples of glacially-sculptured Keweenawan sandstone, red clays, and sand beaches. The Lake Superior sandstone was once the source of a late nineteenth century industry in "brownstone," used for construction in the eastern and mid-western United States.

Among existing landforms are small lakes formed by barrier beaches and a stretch of old-growth hemlock forest extending from a lake beach. Like many of the other islands in the chain, the northern hardwood species on Michigan Island were heavily logged from early settlement days into the 1900s but have since recovered their forest aspect.

Nesting birds on the island include such colonial nesters as double-crested cormorants and great blue herons. White-tailed deer, black bear, snowshoe hare, red fox, and coyote roam the island. Lake trout, whitefish, lake herring, and smelt are part of a commercial and sport fishing industry.

The Conservancy has worked with the National Park Service since 1970 in helping to identify and preserve the scenic and biological resources of Michigan Island.

Protected: 1,481 acres. Northern Wisconsin. Located in Ashland County off the northern coast of the state in Lake Superior. One of 22 islands in the Apostle Islands group belonging to the National Lakeshore. Owned and managed by the National Park Service. For more information contact Superintendent, National Park Service, Apostle Islands National Lakeshore, P.O. Box 729, Bayfield, WI 54814 or call (715) 779-3397.

Renak-Polak Woods

Renak-Polak Woods combines several adjacent tracts of land that together represent one of the last southern mesic hardwood forests in Racine County and one of the best in the state. Large red oak, sugar maple, white ash, and a fine stand of American beech create the deep woods feeling of this preserve. Such "old growth," or near-climax growth, is dominant at Renak-Polak, where a history of sparse logging has created a forest in various stages of succession.

Proximity to the Root River means this preserve is nestled in a setting of sloping ridges and broad valleys. A spring-fed pond on the site produces a stream that flows through the forest. The combination of woods and stream encourages a wealth of plants. As many as 134 species have been identified at Renak-Polak, including many spring ephemerals like hepatica, Dutchman's-breeches, bloodroot, and spring beauty. Rare forest species such as red trillium are also found here.

The Conservancy originally acquired part of the preserve in 1971 through a combination of gifts and purchases. Ownership and management were then transferred to the University of Wisconsin-Parkside. Renak-Polak Woods is a Designated State Natural Area and a significant site for education and research.

Protected: 75 acres. Southeastern Wisconsin. Located in Racine County east of the Root River in Caledonia Township. Designated as a State Natural Area. Several tracts of maple-beech climax woods owned and managed by UW-Parkside. For more information, contact the Department of Life Sciences, UW-Parkside, Kenosha, WI 53140 or call (414) 553-2206.

Rush Creek Bluffs

Rush Creek Bluffs

A diverse array of biological communities characterizes the Rush Creek Bluffs Preserve, making it one of the most remarkable tracts of Wisconsin land bordering the Mississippi. More than 2 miles of limestone-capped bluffs face the river here, parted by crystal-clear Rush Creek as it empties into the larger muddy river's flow. The steep outcroppings are punctuated by dry prairie remnants known as "goat prairies." This site provides a rare example of the few remaining native hillside prairies in the state. Characteristic prairie plants include lead plant, big and little bluestem, blazing star, wood betony, stiff goldenrod and bird-foot violet.

Upland hardwood forest thrives on the north- and east-facing slopes of the bluffs; red and white oak dominate with shagbark hickory, cottonwood, aspen, black walnut, and elm. An understory of dogwood, hazelnut, and woodland herbs and forbs traces the slopes beneath. In the bottomland along the creek, red and silver maples, river birch, willow, and box elder are found. The red-shouldered hawk, a state-threatened species, nests in this riparian forest.

Rush Creek Bluffs continued

Rush Creek itself is a quality trout stream flowing northeast to southwest, fed by a host of springs and streams throughout the preserve. The ecological diversity of Rush Creek Bluffs attracts a variety of wildlife, including white-tailed deer, ruffed grouse, raccoon, muskrat, and beaver. Indian mounds and campsites have also been identified at this site.

Rush Creek Bluffs was acquired by the Conservancy in 1979, then transferred to the Wisconsin Department of Natural Resources for long-term protection and management; it is dedicated as a State Natural Area.

Protected: 1,124.5 acres. Southwestern Wisconsin. Located in Crawford County on the banks of the Mississippi River, northwest of Ferryville. Owned and managed by the Wisconsin Department of Natural Resources. For more information, contact the DNR at 101 S. Webster St., Madison, WI 53707 or call (608) 266-8916.

Toft Point

Toft Point had been protected for generations by the careful foresight of the Toft family. The land was sold to the Conservancy in 1967, thereby achieving the family's longtime wish to preserve a uniquely natural part of Wisconsin. The Conservancy subsequently transferred ownership of Toft Point to the University of Wisconsin-Green Bay, and it is now a study site for many university classes and nature groups.

The value of Toft Point is its high-quality shoreline protected from intensive human activity. Ridges and swales rise along the southeastern portion of the preserve, while a shallow lagoon forms a marshy environment on the northeastern shore. The upland area of Toft Point was once a boreal forest of tall northern trees. Cutting done more than fifty years ago transformed the forest habitat to white pine, white cedar, hemlock, black ash, and balsam fir. Growth is now restoring the boreal character of the land. Forest birds such as the red-breasted nuthatch, winter wren, and olive-sided fly-catcher are characteristic, and the forest floor is home to some rare orchids and other common but beautiful plants. The small-flowered grass-of-Parnassus is found here and in only one other Wisconsin locale.

Protected: 648 acres. Northeastern Wisconsin. Located in Door County along the Lake Michigan shore in Bailey's Harbor Township. Designated as a State Natural Area and a National Natural Landmark. Owned and managed by the University of Wisconsin-Green Bay. For more information, contact College of Environmental Studies, UW-Green Bay, 2420 Nicolet Drive, Green Bay, WI 54301 or call (414) 465-2371.

Appendix A

Table of All Wisconsin Nature Conservancy Preserves and Cooperative Projects (by county)

NA numbers refer to Natural Area designations of the Wisconsin Department of Natural Resources (DNR). For more information on these State Natural Areas, contact the DNR.

County	Site	Acres	Year	Ownership
Adams	Quincy Bluff & Wetlands, NA #272	3,298	1990	TNC=1,665; DNR=1,633
Ashland	Chequamegon Point	45	1988	Private owners
Ashland	Michigan Island	1,481	1970	National Park Service
Ashland/Iron/Rusk	Flambeau River, Upper North Fork	1,112	1985	TNC=51; DNR=1,061
Bayfield	Hixon (Frederick C.) Preserve	392	1982	DNR
Bayfield	Namekagon Preserve	40	1979	Cable Natural History Museum
Bayfield	Porcupine Lake Wilderness	4	1985	Chequamegon National Forest
Bayfield	Port Wing Boreal Forest, NA #154	30	1981	DNR
Bayfield	Squaw Bay	12	1986	Private owners
Brown	Cofrin Arboretum	20	1994	UW–Green Bay
Brown	Point au Sauble	64	1992	TNC
Brown	West Shore Wildlands	314	1970	DNR
Burnett	Olson (Sigurd F.) Memorial Forest	214	1976	Northland College=184; Private owners=30
Chippewa/ Taylor/Manitowoc	Ice Age Trail	1,007	1986	Ice Age Park & Trail Foundation=274; DNR=733
Clark	Schmidt Maple Woods, NA #84	86	1970	UW–Eau Claire Foundation
Columbia	Baraboo River Floodplain Forest, NA #212	27	1985	TNC
Columbia	Otsego Marsh	39	1984	Goose Pond Sanctuary
Columbia	Rowan Creek Fishery	126	1985	DNR
Columbia	Sauk Prairie Eagle Roost	10	1995	Private owners
Crawford	Rush Creek Bluffs, NA #170	1,125	1979	DNR
Crawford	Wauzeka Box Woods	798	1988	DNR
Dane	Black Earth Rettenmund Prairie, NA #210	16	1986	TNC
Dane	Hawk Hill	15	1989	Private owners
Dane	Heritage Heights	5	1971	City of Madison Parks Division
Dane	Kettle Pond	9	1971	City of Madison Parks Division
Dane	UW Arboretum	13	1972	Friends of the Arboretum
Dane	Waubesa Wetlands, NA #114	194	1974	TNC
Dane/Iowa	Thomson Memorial Prairie	175	1964	TNC
Dodge	Neda Mine, NA #144	200	1976	UW Regents
Door	Bailey's Harbor Boreal Forest & Wetlands, NA #284	176	1994	DNR=37; TNC=139
Door	Butts Woods	140	1992	Ridges Sanctuary
Door	Ida Bay Forest	56	1995	TNC
Door	Jackson Harbor Ridges, NA #110	82	1973	Town of Washington Island
Door	Kangaroo Lake	117	1995	TNC= 60; Door County Land Trustees = 57
Door	Mink River Estuary, NA #218	1,465	1977	TNC=1,425; Private owners=40
Door	Ridges Sanctuary, NA #17	126	1962	Ridges Sanctuary
Door	Shivering Sands	192	1992	TNC
Door	Toft Point, NA #57	648	1967	UW–Green Bay=608; TNC=40
Door	Whitefish Dunes State Park, NA #175	80	1977	DNR
Douglas	Brule River	4,958	1981	Private owners
Dunn	Nine Mile Island, NA #236	63	1990	DNR
Florence	Vesley (Albert J.) Estate	40	1984	DNR
Green	Abraham's Woods, NA #38	64	1960	UW–Madison
Green	Muralt Bluff Prairie, NA #139	13	1981	Green County

County	Site	Acres	Year	Ownership
Green	Oliver Prairie, NA #58	5	1962	UW–Madison
Green Lake	Puchyan Prairie, NA #172	120	1981	DNR
Iowa	Anderson (Don) Bottomlands	119	1972	UW–Madison
Iowa	Pine Road Sand Blows	80	1989	DNR
Iron	Bass Lake Preserve, NA #211	840	1980	TNC
Iron	Flambeau Pines & Boreal Forest	60	1987	TNC
Iron/Ashland	Kakagon/Bad River Sloughs	160	1987	Bad River Chippewa
Jackson	North Bend Bottoms	242	1991	DNR
Jefferson	Bean Lake, NA #111	88	1977	DNR
Jefferson	Snapper Prairie, NA #168	28	1979	TNC
Kenosha	Barnes Prairie	6	1988	TNC
Kenosha	Benedict Prairie	6	1962	UW–Milwaukee
Kenosha	Carol Beach	13	1986	DNR
Kenosha	Chiwaukee Prairie, NA #54	191	1965	TNC=115; UW–Parkside=76
Kenosha	Des Plaines River, Upper	443	1989	TNC
Kenosha	Harris (Stanley) Tract	191	1964	UW–Parkside
Kenosha	Kenosha Sand Dunes	56	1994	DNR
Kenosha	Peat Lake, NA #106	171	1972	DNR·
Langlade	Perch Lake	120	1994	DNR
Lincoln	Big Rib River	720	1981	DNR
Lincoln	Menard Isle	333	1983	DNR
Manitowoc	Two Creeks Buried Forest, NA #50	12	1967	DNR
Marinette	Pike River	37	1978	DNR
Marquette	Comstock Marsh, NA #123	240	1974	DNR
Marquette	Muir (John) Memorial Park	27	1986	Marquette County
Marquette	Page Creek Marsh	566	1986	TNC
Marquette	Summerton Bog South	28	1991	TNC
Marquette	Summerton Bog, NA #42	483	1965	TNC
Milwaukee	Milwaukee Arboretum	56	1972	UW–Milwaukee
Milwaukee	Oak Creek	20	1993	Milwaukee County Parks
Oconto	Archibald Lake Hemlock Forest	110	1991	USFS Nicolet Forest
Oconto	Battle Creek Outlet Forest	313	1996	USFS Nicolet Forest
Oneida	Holmboe Conifer Forest, NA #79	32	1965	TNC
Oneida	Spur Lake	73	1996	TNC
Ozaukee	Cedarburg Bog, NA #2	395	1964	UW–Milwaukee=297; DNR=80; TNC=18
Ozaukee	Fairy Chasm, NA #67	20	1970	TNC
Ozaukee	Kurtz Woods, NA #169	31	1979	TNC
Pierce	Alexander Prairie	30	1986	Private owners
Pierce	Rush River Delta, NA #202	119	1974	DNR
Polk	Riegel (Florence Baker) Memorial Park	92	1992	City of St. Croix Falls
Portage	Buena Vista Marsh	240	1971	Dane County Conservation League=200; DNR=40
Portage	Dewey Marsh, NA #182	80	1990	DNR
Racine	Ranger Mac's Fen	33	1968	UW–Parkside
Racine	Renak-Polak Woods, NA #95	75	1971	UW–Parkside
Richland	Hub City Bog, NA #80	50	1970	UW Regents
Rock	Newark Road Prairie, NA #113	33	1973	Beloit College
Sauk	Ableman's Gorge, NA #75	16	1968	UW–Madison
Sauk	Baraboo Hills–East	120	1992	TNC
Sauk	Baxter's Hollow, NA #82	4,208	1969	TNC=4,174; Private owners=33.5
Sauk	Bear Creek Cave, NA #126	45	1975	UW–Madison
Sauk	Devils Lake State Park	143	1991	DNR=0.18; TNC=142.5

Appendix A continued

County	Site	Acres	Year	Ownership
Sauk	Durst Rockshelter, NA #44	40	1965	TNC
Sauk	Ferry Bluff, NA #217	65	1975	TNC=64; Eagle Valley Environmentalists=1
Sauk	Freedom Woods Forest HCA	491	1996	TNC
Sauk	Gasser Sand Barrens	3	1970	TNC
Sauk	Hartmann Site	46	1980	DNR
Sauk	Hemlock Draw	543	1964	TNC
Sauk	Honey Creek, NA #91	478	1969	TNC=398; Private owners=80
Sauk	Leopold Memorial Woods	80	1967	TNC
Sauk	Lodde's Mill Bluff, NA #52	35	1963	UW–Madison
Sauk	Morgan Hone Preserve	79	1987	TNC
Sauk	Pan Hollow	131	1970	TNC
Sauk	Pewit's Nest, NA #200	27	1991	DNR
Sauk	Pine Hollow, NA #45	381	1964	TNC
Sauk	Schluckebier Sand Prairie	23	1970	TNC
Sauk	South Bluff Oak Forest	159	1971	TNC
Sauk	Spring Green Preserve, NA #102	590	1971	TNC=429; Private owners=161
Sauk/Iowa/Richland	Lower Wisconsin River State Forest	191	1986	DNR
Shawano	Jung Hemlock & Beech Forest, NA #129	80	1976	DNR
Sheboygan	Muehl Springs	75	1986	TNC
Sheboygan	Sheboygan County Memorial Arboretum	34	1970	UW–Sheboygan
St. Croix	Apple River Canyon, NA #145	115	1980	DNR
St. Croix	St. Croix Island Wildlife Area	80	1983	DNR
Trempealeau	Decorah Mounds	40	1976	TNC
Trempealeau	Sacia Memorial Ridge	29	1975	TNC
Vilas	Crab Lake Preserve	130	1991	Crab Lake Conservation Foundation
Vilas	Lake Mary	42	1990	DNR
Vilas	Warwick Woods	108	1980	DNR
Walworth	Beulah Bog, NA #122	62	1975	DNR
Walworth	Hoganson (Les & Jane) Preserve	219	1984	TNC
Walworth	Peterkin Pond	128	1990	DNR
Walworth	Pickerel Lake Fen, NA #209	47	1985	TNC=39; Private owners=8
Walworth/Waukesha	Lulu Lake, NA #138	1,048	1986	DNR=207, Private owners=210, TNC=631
Washburn	Fried-Sarona Woods	160	1970	UW–Eau Claire Foundation
Washburn	Fried-Sunfish Lake Forest	69	1970	UW–Eau Claire Foundation
Washington	Loew's Lake	255	1989	DNR
Washington	Thiemann (Douglas H.) Arboretum	7	1970	UW–Milwaukee
Washington	Zinn (Walter & Rose) Preserve	227	1981	TNC
Waukesha	Cooling's Meadow Preserve	30	1981	Waukesha County
Waukesha	Falk Woods	58	1973	Waukesha County
Waukesha	Genesee Oak Opening, NA #153	51	1979	DNR
Waukesha	Greene (Howard T.) Site	62	1973	Carroll College
Waukesha	Haffner Oak Opening	8	1995	TNC
Waukesha	Holz Island	3	1971	City of Muskego
Waukesha	Martin's Woods	32	1993	Waukesha Land Conservancy
Waukesha	Nelson Oak Woods	114	1972	Waukesha Land Conservancy
Waukesha	Reuss Pines	5	1969	UW–Milwaukee
Waupaca	Bear Creek Wetland	75	1995	Waupaca County
Waupaca	Cactus Rock, NA #43	11	1965	Lawrence University
Winnebago	Hi-Trestle Woods	10	1966	UW–Oshkosh Foundation
Winnebago	Omro Prairie	5	1975	TNC
Winnebago/ Fond du Lac	Gromme (Owen & Anne) Preserve	608	1988	TNC

Total Acreage **38,185**

Appendix B

Endangered and Threatened Plants and Animals in Wisconsin

Wisconsin Endangered Species: Any species whose continued existence as a viable component of this state's wild animals or wild plants is determined by the Department to be in jeopardy on the basis of scientific evidence.

Wisconsin Threatened Species:
Any species which appears likely, within the foreseeable future, on the basis of scientific evidence to become endangered.

**Federally Endangered Species: Any species or subspecies which is in danger of extinction throughout all or a significant portion of its range.

*Federally Threatened Species: Any species or subspecies which is likely within the foreseeable future to become endangered throughout all or a significant portion of its range.

Mammals

Endangered

**Timber wolf *(Canis lupus)*
Canada lynx *(Lynx canadensis)*
Pine marten *(Martes americana)*

Threatened

None

Birds

Endangered

Barn owl *(Tyto alba)*
Bewick's wren *(Thryomanes bewickii)*
Caspian tern *(Sterna caspia)*
Common tern *(Sterna hirundo)*
Forster's tern *(Sterna forsteri)*
Loggerhead shrike *(Lanius ludovicianus)*
**Peregrine falcon *(Falco peregrinus)*
**Piping plover *(Charadrius melodus)*
Trumpeter swan *(Cygnus buccinator)*
Worm-eating warbler *(Helmitheros vermivorus)*
Yellow-throated warbler *(Dendroica dominica)*

Threatened

Acadian flycatcher *(Empidonax virescens)*
*Bald eagle *(Haliaeetus leucocephalus)*
Bell's vireo *(Vireo bellii)*
Cerulean warbler *(Dendroica cerulea)*
Great egret *(Casmerodius albus)*
Greater prairie-chicken *(Tympanuchus cupido pinnatus)*
Hooded warbler *(Wilsonia citrina)*
Kentucky warbler *(Oporornis formosus)*
Osprey *(Pandion haliaetus)*
Red-necked grebe *(Podiceps grisegena)*

Red-shouldered hawk *(Buteo lineatus)*
Yellow-crowned night-heron *(Nycticorax violaceus)*

Reptiles & Amphibians

Endangered

Blanchard's cricket frog *(Acris crepitans)*
Massasauga *(Sistrurus catenatus)*
Northern ribbon snake *(Thamnophis sauritus)*
Ornate box turtle *(Terrapene ornata)*
Queen snake *(Regina septemvittata)*
Slender glass lizard *(Ophisaurus attenuatus)*
Western ribbon snake *(Thamnophis proximus)*

Threatened

Blanding's turtle *(Emydoidea blandingi)*
Wood turtle *(Clemmys insculpta)*

Fishes

Endangered

Bluntnose darter *(Etheostoma chlorosomum)*
Crystal darter *(Ammocrypta asprella)*
Goldeye *(Hiodon alosoides)*
Gravel chub *(Hybopsis x-punctata)*
Pallid shiner *(Notropis amnis)*
Skipjack herring *(Alosa chrysochloris)*
Slender madtom *(Noturus exilis)*
Starhead topminnow *(Fundulus notti)*
Striped shiner *(Notropis chrysocephalus)*

Threatened

Black buffalo *(Ictiobus niger)*
Blue sucker *(Cycleptus elongatus)*
Gilt darter *(Percina evides)*
Greater redhorse *(Moxostoma valenciennesi)*

Longear sunfish *(Lepomis megalotis)*
Ozark minnow *(Dionda nubila)*
Paddlefish *(Polyodon spathula)*
Pugnose shiner *(Notropis anogenus)*
Redfin shiner *(Notropis umbratilis)*
River redhorse *(Moxostoma carinatum)*
Speckled chub *(Hybopsis aestivalis)*

Insects

Endangered

Extra-striped snaketail dragonfly *(Ophiogomphus anomalus)*
Flat-headed mayfly *(Anepeorus simplex)*
**Giant carrion beetle *(Nicrophorus americanus)*
Knobel's riffle beetle *(Stenelmis knobeli)*
Northern blue butterfly *(Lycaeides idas)*
Pecatonica river mayfly *(Acanthametropus pecatonica)*
Phlox moth *(Schinia indiana)*
Powesheik skipper *(Oarisma powesheik)*
Pygmy snaketail dragonfly *(Ophiogomphus howei)*
Silphium borer moth *(Papaipema silphii)*

Threatened

Frosted elfin *(Incisalia irus)*
Regal fritillary *(Speyeria idalia)*
Swamp metalmark *(Calephelis muticum)*

Snails

Endangered

Hubricht's vertigo *(Vertigo hubrichti)*
Occult vertigo *(Vertigo occulta)*

Threatened

Cherrystone drop *(Hendersonia occulta)*
Wing snaggletooth *(Gastrocopta procera)*

Mussels

Endangered

Bullhead *(Plethobasus cyphyus)*
Butterfly *(Ellipsaria lineolata)*
Ebony shell *(Fusconaia ebena)*
Elephant ear *(Elliptio crassidens)*
**Higgins' eye pearly mussel *(Lampsilis higginsi)*
Purple wartyback *(Cyclonaias tuberculata)*
Rainbow shell *(Villosa iris)*

Snuffbox *(Epioblasma triquetra)*
Spectacle case *(Cumberlandia monodonta)*
**Winged mapleleaf *(Quadrula fragosa)*
Yellow & slough sandshell *(Lampsilis teres)*

Threatened

Buckhorn *(Tritogonia verrucosa)*
Ellipse *(Actinonaias ellipsiformis)*
Monkeyface *(Quadrula metanevra)*
Rock pocketbook *(Arcidens confragosus)*
Salamander mussel *(Simpsonaias ambigua)*
Slippershell *(Alasmidonta viridis)*
Wartyback *(Quadrula nodulata)*

Plants

Endangered

Alpine milk vetch *(Astragalus alpinus)*
Angle-stemmed spikerush *(Eleocharis quadrangulata)*
Auricled twayblade *(Listera auriculata)*
Beak grass *(Diarrhena americana)*
Blue-stemmed goldenrod *(Solidago caesia)*
Bog rush *(Juncus stygius)*
Brook grass *(Catabrosa aquatica)*
Butterwort *(Pinguicula vulgaris)*
Carolina anemone *(Anemone caroliniana)*
Chestnut sedge *(Fimbristylis puberula)*
Cooper's milk vetch *(Astragalus neglectus)*
Crow-spur sedge *(Carex crus-corvi)*
Dotted blazing star *(Liatris punctata)*
Dwarf bilberry *(Vaccinium cespitosum)*
Fassett's locoweed(Oxytropis campestris)*
Floating marsh marigold *(Caltha natans)*
Foamflower *(Tiarella cordifolia)*
Goblin fern *(Botrychium mormo)*
Great white lettuce *(Prenanthes crepidinea)*
Green spleenwort *(Asplenium viride)*
Hairy meadow parsnip *(Thaspium barbinode)*
Harbinger-of-spring *(Erigenia bulbosa)*
Heart-leaved plantain *(Plantago cordata)*
Hemlock-parsley *(Conioselinum chinense)*
Hop-like sedge *(Carex lupuliformis)*
Hudson Bay anemone *(Anemone multifida)*
Intermediate sedge *(Carex media)*
Lake cress *(Armoracia lacustris)*
Lake Huron tansy *(Tanacetum huronense)*
Lanceolate whitlow-cress *(Draba lanceolata)*
Lapland rosebay *(Rhododendron lapponicum)*
Large-leaved sandwort *(Arenaria macrophylla)*

Moonwort (*Botrychium lunaria*)
Mountain cranberry (*Vaccinium vitis-idaea*)
Netted nut-rush (*Scleria reticularis*)
Northern commandra (*Geocaulon lividum*)
Pale false foxglove (*Agalinus skinneriana*)
Pine-drops (*Pterospora andromedea*)
Pink milkwort (*Polygala incarnata*)
*Prairie bush clover(*Lespedeza leptostachya*)
Prairie plum (*Astragalus crassicarpus*)
*Prairie white-fringed orchid(*Platanthera leucophaea*)
Purple milkweed (*Asclepias purpurascens*)
Rough white lettuce (*Prenanthes aspera*)
Sand dune willow (*Salix cordata*)
Sand violet (*Viola fimbriatula*)
Seaside crowfoot (*Ranunculus cymbalaria*)
Selago-like spikemoss (*Selaginella selaginoides*)
Small shinleaf (*Pyrola minor*)
Small skullcap (*Scutellaria parvula*)
Small yellow water crowfoot (*Ranunculus gmelinii*)
Small-flowered grass-of-parnassus (*Parnassia parviflora*)
Smith melic grass (*Melica smithii*)
Smooth phlox (*Phlox glaberrima*)
Spotted pondweed (*Potamogeton pulcher*)
Squashberry (*Viburnum edule*)
Stoneroot (*Collinsonia canadensis*)
Tussock bulrush (*Scirpus cespitosus*)
Umbrella sedge (*Fuirena pumila*)
Wild hyacinth (*Camassia scilloides*)
Wild petunia (*Ruellia humilis*)

Threatened

Algal-leaved pondweed (*Potamogeton confervoides*)
Bald rush (*Psilocarya scirpoides*)
Beaked spike rush (*Eleocharis rostellata*)
Beautiful sedge (*Carex concinna*)
Bladderpod (*Lesquerella ludoviciana*)
Blue ash (*Fraxinus quadrangulata*)
Bog bluegrass (*Poa paludigena*)
Braun's holly fern (*Polystichum braunii*)
Brittle prickly pear (*Opuntia fragilis*)
Broad-leaved twayblade (*Listera convallarioides*)
Calypso orchid (*Calypso bulbosa*)
Carey's sedge (*Carex careyana*)
Clustered broomrape (*Orobanche fasciculata*)
Coast sedge (*Carex exilis*)
Drooping sedge (*Carex prasina*)
Dune goldenrod (*Solidago spathulata*)
*Dune thistle(*Cirsium pitcheri*)
*Dwarf lake iris(*Iris lacustris*)
English sundew (*Drosera anglica*)

False asphodel (*Tofieldia glutinosa*)
Forked aster (*Aster furcatus*)
Garber's sedge (*Carex garberi*)
Handsome sedge (*Carex formosa*)
Hawthorn-leaved gooseberry (*Ribes oxyacanthoides*)
Kitten tails (*Besseya bullii*)
Lenticular sedge (*Carex lenticularis*)
Linear-leaved sundew (*Drosera linearis*)
Marsh grass-of-Parnassus (*Parnassia palustris*)
Marsh valerian (*Valeriana sitchensis*)
Michaux's sedge (*Carex michauxiana*)
Muskroot (*Adoxa moschatellina*)
New England violet (*Viola novae-angliae*)
*Northern monkshood(*Aconitum noveboracense*)
Pinnatifid spleenwort (*Asplenium pinnatifidum*)
Prairie Indian plantain (*Cacalia tuberosa*)
Prairie milkweed (*Asclepias sullivantii*)
Prairie thistle (*Cirsium hillii*)
Prairie-parsley (*Polytaenia nuttallii*)
Purple coneflower (*Echinacea pallida*)
Ram's-head lady's-slipper (*Cypripedium arietinum*)
Round fruited St. Johns wort (*Hypericum sphaerocarpum*)
Round stemmed false foxglove (*Agalinus gattingeri*)
Sand reed (*Calamovilfa longifolia*)
Sheathed pondweed (*Potamogeton vaginatus*)
Slender bush clover (*Lespedeza virginica*)
Small round-leaved orchis (*Amerorchis rotundifolia*)
Snow trillium (*Trillium nivale*)
Spike trisetum (*Trisetum spicatum*)
Sweet coltsfoot (*Petasites sagittatus*)
Thickspike wheatgrass (*Elymus lanceolatus* ssp. *psammophilus*)
Tubercled orchid (*Platanthera flava*)
Western fescue (*Festuca occidentalis*)
White lady's-slipper (*Cypripedium candidum*)
Wild quinine (*Parthenium integrifolium*)
Wooly milkweed (*Asclepias lanuginosa*)
Yellow giant hyssop (*Agastache nepetoides*)
Yellowish gentian (*Gentiana alba*)

This list was provided to The Nature Conservancy by:

Wisconsin Bureau of Endangered Resources
Department of Natural Resources
P.O. Box 7921
Madison, WI 53707-7921

Index